WORDS FOR BIRDS

Sálim Ali

WORDS FOR BIRDS

The Collected Radio Broadcasts

edited by

TARA GANDHI

black kite
AN IMPRINT OF PERMANENT BLACK

in association with

ASHOKA UNIVERSITY

Words for Birds, first published in hardback 2021
by Black Kite (an imprint of Permanent Black)

in association with

ASHOKA UNIVERSITY

and

Hachette India
(an Hachette UK company)

All editorial management by Black Kite

978-93-91028-299

10 9 8 7 6 5 4 3 2

Black Kite/Permanent Black, D28 Oxford Apartments,
11 IP Extension, Delhi 110092

Printed in India by Manipal Technologies Limited, Manipal

The royalties from this book go to the Sálim Ali Nature Conservation Fund (SANCF) of the Bombay Natural History Society.

Contents

PART III: LEARNING ABOUT BIRDS

PART IV: BIRDS AT RISK

PART V: NATURE IN INDIA

Acknowledgements

The foremost acknowledgement for this collection goes to All India Radio, the first broadcaster of each of these talks. Their effort in spreading knowledge of nature in India through the words of Sálim Ali is appreciated with gratitude.

The Bombay Natural History Society (BNHS), my alma mater, is a repository of the works of Sálim Ali. This collection of texts of his radio talks is sourced entirely from their archives of digitised copies of his meticulously catalogued original papers. A number of the photographs in this book are sourced from this archive. My sincere thanks to Dr Deepak Apte, former Director of the BNHS, for providing me access to this treasury of papers and images and for facilitating my work. Mrs Nirmala Reddy Barure, the Librarian, was always helpful, patiently searching out the documents I required. A special thanks to Dr Mahmood Alam for translating portions of Sálim Ali's Hindustani broadcast.

I am grateful to Rukun Advani for always encouraging me to work on compiling Dr Sálim Ali's writings and for offering to publish this collection as a book.

I benefited from conversations with Ramachandra Guha, who gave me valuable advice on working with archival material. Sumaira Abdulali and Zai Whitaker, both members of Dr Sálim Ali's family and my good friends, generously welcomed this project and indulged my stream of questions on their recollections of his life. Asad Rahmani and Aasheesh Pittie were ready with their help to source the pictures and documents I needed. My husband Gopalkrishna was a constant support by my side while most of this work was done during the distressing time of the COVID-19 pandemic of 2020–21.

Having had the unparalleled privilege of being Dr Sálim Ali's student, this has been a journey of discovery. Some years back, while going through files of his papers and documents in the Nehru Memorial Museum and Library, I came across several typewritten lists of his books, his scientific articles, general interest writings, etc. Among these I found a list titled "Radio Talks". I put it aside – only to re-discover it lately. It was a particular joy for me to go through the scripts of his talks and to see the notes and corrections in the beautifully clear handwriting that I knew so well. Reading his accounts of birds and nature brought back memories of many road trips and walks with him when he visited my field-study sites, during which his conversations were elevating and educative. I am fortunate to have had first-hand experience of the wisdom and teaching of a great scientist and exceptional personality. This book is dedicated to the memory of Dr Sálim Ali, my teacher and mentor, in honour of his 125th birth anniversary.

Chronology of Sálim Ali's Broadcasts

1 Birds: A National Asset (Broadcast from Lahore, 2 December 1941)

2 Birds: The International Wayfarers (Broadcast from Lahore, 28 December 1941)

3 Bird Watching (Bombay, 7 March 1942)

4 Further Experiences in Bird Watching (Bombay, 14 March 1942)

5 Birds in August (Bombay, 28 July 1942)

6 Birds in September (Bombay, School Broadcast, 18 August 1942)

7 Birds in October (Bombay, School Broadcast, 29 September 1942)

8 The Monsoon Comes: Bird Life (Bombay, 29 June 1946)

9a *Chand Hairat Angez Paradon aur Janwaron ke Char – Chand Bare aur Chhote Ghonsla Bananewale* (Bombay, School Broadcast, 9 October 1946)

9b Some Amazing Homes of Birds and Animals (1946; translation of 9a)

10 Bird Study in India (Delhi, 19 July 1947)

11 Courtship and Display Among Birds (The Kingdom of Birds Series, Delhi, 6 September 1947)

12 How I Became Interested in Birds (Singapore, 15 March 1950)

13 Answering Questions about Birds (Bombay, 4 February 1951)

14 Bird Watching (Bombay, 8 January 1952)

15 The Fauna of India (Bombay, for External Service, Delhi, 12 November 1952)

16 Wildlife Preservation in Kashmir (Bombay, 17 November 1952)

17 Interview with Dr Bernhard Rensch (15 March 1953)

18 Birding in Sikkim (Bombay, 20 March 1953)

19 The Birds of Sikkim (Bombay, 20 March 1953)

20 Some Interesting Animals of Sikkim (10 August 1953)

21 Trends in Modern Bird Study (Bombay, 20 September 1955)

22 The Preservation of Wild Birds (Bombay, 18 October 1955)

23 Bird Life of the Chilka Lake (Bombay, for Cuttack Station, 4 November 1955)

24 The "Bird Wing" and Bird Preservation in India (Bombay, 6 October 1956)

25 The Vanishing Species (22 April 1957)

26 The Flamingo (Bombay, 9 July 1957)

27 The Alien Migrants (Bombay, 6 August 1957)

Introduction

Sálim Ali's passion for birds spanned most of the ninety-one years of his life. Even as a boy, he took every opportunity to look for birds, though his interest at the time was to shoot them with his treasured airgun and have them cooked for a snack. This childish mischief was to eventually develop into a lifelong pursuit of ornithology and nature conservation. This is how it began: "On one of my rare occasions of successful murder I noticed that the victim, which was intended to be a common House Sparrow, bore a curious yellow patch on the throat." He took the little dead bird to the Bombay Natural History Society (BNHS) to find out more about it and was told it was in fact not the common house sparrow but a rarer variety – a Yellow-throated Sparrow (*Petronia xanthocollis*). From then on, "like ripples from a pebble dropped in water the circles of my interest in ornithology widened."[1]

Sálim Ali came from a privileged background. His distinguished Bombay ancestors included a president of the Indian National Congress and a member of the Indian Civil Service. The young Sálim was not particularly interested in or good at his books, though he says he "had dreamed of taking up zoology, particularly ornithology as a profession when I grew up and of becoming an intrepid explorer and big-game hunter."[2] Hunting wildlife

[1] Radio talk: "How I Became Interested in Birds" (1950).

[2] Sálim Ali, *The Fall of a Sparrow* (Delhi: Oxford University Press, 1985).

alongside elders and friends was fashionable and an accepted practice in the early-twentieth century, and he revelled in it for a while before being sent off to Burma (Myanmar) as a teenager to work for his family's mining and timber business. After a few years of this he did a course in commercial law and accountancy, then again worked in his family's cotton-exporting business as a clerk.

Through all this time, Sálim Ali kept in touch with the BNHS, spending hours in its library and "rummaging among the bird collection" to learn more about Indian birds.[3] It was only when he was about thirty that he got his first opportunity to work in his favourite terrain. In 1926 he was appointed as a guide lecturer in the Natural History Section of the Prince of Wales Museum in Bombay (now Chhatrapati Shivaji Maharaj Vastu Sangrahalaya), which proved to be his breakthrough into the world of ornithology. After three years he tired of this rather repetitive job and decided to undergo serious taxonomic and field-based ornithological training at the Berlin University Museum, where he learnt from inspirational teachers about the life histories of birds and their migratory patterns. His fascination now became his profession – the study of the live bird in its natural surroundings alongside biogreography, ecology, and the science of ethology.

After his return to India in 1930, Sálim Ali's childhood dream of becoming an explorer came true. Supported by the BNHS, princely families, and other benefactors, he took on large-scale bird surveys all over the country. Covering the humid rainforests of the Western Ghats in the south, the snow-capped Himalaya in the north, the arid salt marsh of the Rann of Kutch in the extreme west, through central India to the great Chilika lake in the east, he trod the length and breadth of India. An arduous trans-Himalayan trek involved crossing the 16,750-foot-high Lipu Lekh Pass to the Tibetan plateau, to "study the natural conditions

[3] Ibid.

under which birds live on the Roof of the World, to ascertain at first hand what species breed in the area."[4] The many books he wrote on India's birds were based on these expeditions.[5] The *Book of Indian Birds* (1941) became a bestseller and made him famous. The monumental ten-volume *Handbook of the Birds of India and Pakistan*, co-authored with his long-time American associate S. Dillon Ripley, emerged from his meticulous observations and bird collections. Numerous scientific papers that he wrote were based on his own research and from the findings of major projects he led, such as the "BNHS–WHO Bird Migration Study Project" and the "Ecological Study of Bird Hazards at Indian Aerodromes". For general readers he wrote a number of articles for popular magazines and newsletters.

The BNHS, which was the domain of British sportsmen, amateur birdwatchers, specimen collectors, and nature enthusiasts, passed to Indian hands after Independence. Sálim Ali was appointed its curator and secretary, and eventually took over as its president, heading the organisation for the rest of his life. Under his leadership the BNHS progressed from a rather sporty club to a prestigious research and nature-conservation institution.

As the political situation in India changed after British rule ended and new laws were established, Sálim Ali adapted and modified his own views. This is evident from the chronology of his radio talks. Though he had enjoyed the occasional shikar during his younger days, when hunting was permitted, he now vehemently condemned the poaching of rare animals such as rhinos. He was vocal also against the "enormous holocausts" caused by the

[4] "An Ornithological Pilgrimage to Lake Manasarowar and Mount Kailas", *Journal of the Bombay Natural History Society*, 1946.

[5] Books by Sálim Ali: *The Birds of Kutch, Indian Hill Birds, Birds of Kerala, The Birds of Sikkim, Field Guide to the Birds of the Eastern Himalayas, Handbook of the Birds of India and Pakistan* (co-authored with S. Dillon Ripley), *Common Birds* (co-authored with Laeeq Futehally), and *The Fall of a Sparrow.*

"gargantuan shoots" of migratory birds in wetlands,[6] and the "despicable gangs of slaughterers" who hunted breeding egrets for their beautiful feathers in demand for the Western fashion industry.[7] It may seem surprising to find him speaking of the need for "facilities for controlled big-game hunting",[8] and of the "exhilarating" experience of markhor and ibex hunting.[9] But he eventually set aside his belief that well-regulated sport-hunting was not harmful and gave up hunting altogether, in full agreement with the legal ban on killing wildlife. This apparent inconsistency between Sálim Ali's earlier and later opinion is best explained in his autobiography: "I have admitted elsewhere I have been an avid hunter in my time and gave up not as an act of contrition but for a more pragmatic reason – namely the all-round deterioration of the wildlife position in our country, with many species being pushed to the verge of extinction."[10] The evolution of his views over the years was in step with the times and is even more relevant today, being directly related to the serious decline in bird and animal populations and the degradation of natural ecosystems in the country.

In the post-independence era in India, Sálim Ali became an influential figure for wildlife conservation. Though well known as the "Greatest Indian Ornithologist" or as "India's Birdman", his contribution as a great conservationist is less well recognised. Sanctuaries and wildlife-protected areas were created after he convinced those in power of the merits of instituting legal protection for crucial ecosystems and wildlife habitats. He persuaded Prime Minister Jawaharlal Nehru to make the Bharatpur wetland in Rajasthan

[6] Ali, *The Fall of a Sparrow*.

[7] Radio talk: "Preservation of Wild Birds" (1955).

[8] Radio talk: "The Fauna of India" (1952).

[9] Radio talk: "Wildlife Preservation in Kashmir" (1952).

[10] Excerpt from *The Fall of a Sparrow*, reproduced in the anthology *A Bird's Eye View*, ed. Tara Gandhi (Ranikhet: Permanent Black 2007).

a bird sanctuary, which now has the status of a National Park; later, at his behest Indira Gandhi was instrumental in saving the Silent Valley rainforest in Kerala. He influenced policy-makers to establish protected areas for endangered species in many parts of the country. Though he received numerous national and international awards, including honorary doctorates, and was honoured by the Government of India with a Padma Vibhushan in 1976 and nominated as a member of the Rajya Sabha in 1985, he never involved himself in politics and couldn't resist the occasional dig at politicians who, he said, "hold forth so glibly . . . [but] unfortunately only display their ignorance of the finely balanced interplay that exists among God's creatures."[11]

An excellent communicator, Sálim Ali reached out to a cross-section of people – schoolchildren, young scientists, senior executives, politicians, maharajas – to convey the importance of conservation and the beauty and joy of nature. The eminent ecologist Madhav Gadgil says of Sálim Ali that he was "the man who taught Indians to appreciate, to study at first hand, to treasure, to work towards conserving the rich living heritage of this country."

This collection is compiled from a list titled "Radio Talks" that was in all likelihood prepared by Sálim Ali himself. Scanned copies of the talks dated from 1941 to 1980 were in the archives of the BNHS, except for two: "Birds in July" (1942) and "Keoladeo National Park" (1982). These two could not be traced despite a thorough search. The last talk in the present collection, "Watching Birds" (1985), was not in the list but the scanned text was in the library.

The collection includes a Hindustani broadcast for schools and is evidence of Sálim Ali's considerable communication skills.[12] He says: "The object of these talks is really to interest listeners, in the

[11] Radio talk: "Some Interesting Animals of Sikkim" (1953).

[12] Radio talk: "*Chand Hairat Angez Parandon aur Janwaron ke Ghar – chand bare aur chhote ghonsla bananewale*" (1946).

first instance for the healthy pleasure and satisfaction bird watching affords rather than for its intrinsic scientific possibilities."[13] His desire to make people understand that birds have a crucial place in nature's cyclic processes, that they are beneficial to agriculture, and that they contribute to the country's economy comes through powerfully. Valuable insights can also be found on the many changes in India's bird life over the years and of the declining population and geographic range of various wild animals that were abundant during his time. Today, vultures are a rare sight, whereas in 1951 Sálim Ali says: "At any time of the day vultures may be seen in the sky";[14] and while the Himalayan Black Bear is an uncommon and vulnerable species now, in 1952 he found bears so prolific in Kashmir that he recommended controlling their numbers.[15]

The talks cover a wide spectrum of topics and are presented in an elegantly conversational yet highly informative and educative style intended to capture the attention of radio listeners – and now book readers as well.

Important conservation messages and scientific data are interspersed with characteristic touches of humour – sometimes self-deprecating – such as when he says he looked like a "distinctly shabby khaki-clad garage mechanic type";[16] or expressively lyrical, as in his description of sunbirds – "they flit about from flower to flower like gems in the sunshine";[17] or by capturing a musical call – "the merry tinkling warble of the fantail flycatcher".[18]

While his focus is largely on birds, it is evident from the subjects of these talks that Sálim Ali was interested in all forms of wildlife.

[13] Radio talk: "Bird Watching" (1942).
[14] Radio talk: "Answering Questions about Birds" (1951).
[15] Radio talk: "Wildlife Preservation in Kashmir" (1952).
[16] Radio talk: "Watching Birds" (1985).
[17] Radio talk: "Birds in September" (1942).
[18] Radio talk: "Birds in Summer" (1963).

His repeated plea for scientific management and the science-based conservation of ecosystems and true wildernesses is particularly notable. He was troubled by the country's huge population growth, on account of which forests were being converted to farmlands and human habitation. When this resulted in human conflict with wild animals, he sympathised with the farmers whose crops were damaged by elephants, deer, or wild pigs,[19] even as he spoke out against mismanagement and the destruction of natural habitats: "Whatever method we employ, the intellectual or the physical or a combination of both, time is running out for man. He must realise that his body, like that of other animals, is subject to narrow physical and chemical constraints and that, however intellectually versatile he may be, he could become a victim of ecological disaster just as any other animal if he refuses to pay heed to the warnings of a misused natural system working under fixed natural laws. To us in India especially, this is the writing on the wall."[20]

Sálim Ali wanted to inspire and excite young people to enjoy being close to nature out in the wilderness, and to share the wonder and delights of bird watching. Despite his phenomenal knowledge, he had the humility of the best kind of scientist, never claiming to know all the answers: "Indeed some of the mysteries connected with the migration of birds seem hardly likely ever to be solved."[21] It is this spirit of enquiry that he wished to inculcate in listeners and readers.

Delivered over almost half a century, between 1941 and 1985, these talks were recorded mostly at the All India Radio (AIR) station in Bombay (Mumbai), for broadcast from there, as well

[19] Radio talk: "The Fauna of India" (1952).
[20] Radio talk: "Man and Nature in India" (1976).
[21] Radio talk: "Trends in Modern Bird Study" (1955).

as from stations in other cities, including from the Lahore station in 1941 in undivided India. One talk was broadcast from Singapore and refers to his friend and benefactor W.T. Loke. Sálim Ali sometimes used portions of the scripts in his articles, and occasionally introduced excerpts from his writings into his talks. While these shorter writings have been collected and published earlier,[22] this book is, to the best of my knowledge, the first exclusive collection of the texts of his radio broadcasts.

The script of each talk was typed out on an old-fashioned typewriter, then edited by hand with a fine-nibbed pen in his artistic, almost calligraphic, and perfectly legible handwriting. Each was about 1500 words, timed to last fourteen minutes when read out. He was quite particular about this, as seen from his notes in the margins, such as, "should be 20 lines shorter", "too long, to be pruned", "finished in 8 minutes!" Date, time, recording station, as well as the station from which each talk was intended to be broadcast were also meticulously noted on the top margin of every draft.

In this book, thirty-five talks are separated into five broadly topical sections. Within each section the talks are arranged in chronological order, and a full chronology of the broadcasts spread over more than forty years has been provided. The recording studio, date of recording, and where indicated, the place from which the talk was to be broadcast are given in the footnotes. One of the talks was delivered in conversational Hindustani, for which the text had originally been typed in the Roman script. This has now been copied from Sálim Ali's original and included along with a translation.[23]

[22] Though his essays are much anthologised, the collected shorter writings are in *A Bird's Eye View*, ed. Tara Gandhi (Ranikhet: Permanent Black 2007).

[23] Radio talk: "*Chand Hairat Angez Parandon aur Janwaron ke Ghar – chand bare aur chhote ghonsla bananewale*" (1946) translated as "Some Amazing Homes of Birds and Animals".

While reading each section, it will be noticed that there is often a fair amount of repetition. Sometimes, entire paragraphs are reproduced in more than one talk within a section, as also in those across sections, wherever they were relevant. Particular nuggets recur – Sálim Ali favourites frequently repeated are the Baya weaver bird's breeding behaviour, bird migration, and birds as agents of agricultural pest control. Each talk was composed carefully as an autonomous piece for different audiences to be broadcast from varying locations. The repetitions have not, therefore, been edited out, nor have any of the scripts been modified – to have done so would have compromised the integrity of each piece and tampered with the flow of the talk. The scripts are all reproduced exactly as they were written for delivery. The names of birds, and of places that have since been renamed (e.g. Bombay, now Mumbai), as well as lesser-known alternatives used such as "Kinchinjunga" have been replicated as found in the original to retain the flavour of the times. Since each talk is whole and distinct and reads like a short essay, this book need not necessarily be read sequentially from start to finish. The reader can dip into it in any order to be hugely educated and entertained.

PART I

LOOKING AT BIRDS

"Fifty years ago bird watching in India was nowhere as popular, or indeed respectable, as it has become today"

– Sálim Ali, Radio Talk, "Watching Birds" (1985)

Equipped for birdwatching, Bharatpur.
(*Photo from the BNHS archives*)

Recording hill birds
(*Photo from the BNHS archives*)

1

Bird Watching*

Time and again in the course of my experience as a bird-watcher, I have fallen in with persons who have left me with a feeling, as they withdraw, that they were inwardly tapping a pitying finger on their foreheads. Their first glimpse of me very often has, it is true, been of a distinctly shabby khaki-clad individual of the garage mechanic type, wandering leisurely and rather aimlessly about the countryside and surreptitiously peeping into bushes, and holes in tree-trunks and earth banks. At times they have seen me becoming suddenly rooted to the ground with a pair of ponderous-looking binoculars glued to my eyes for long stretches of time. I doubt not that some of them have suspected all these hole-and-corner tactics to be conducted on behalf of some foreign power with nefarious designs. Curiosity – or it may be the thrill of confronting a dangerous criminal caught in the act – sometimes draws them closer to me, and frequently an amiable but rather vague conversation ensues. My new acquaintance is usually left unconvinced. The distance between us slowly increases, and the next time I turn round he has vanished.

Watching birds? Surely sane people don't do that: Do you kill and eat them? No? Do you catch them and cage them, and teach

*7 March 1942, Bombay.

them to talk or turn somersaults? No? Do you sell them or export them, dead or alive, whole or in parts? Do you make medicines out of them, or how else do you convert them into hard cash? "Well, if it is none of these things," I imagine them saying to themselves, "then surely our suspicion was correct. Let's move on before he turns violent." And in this they are probably wise. I remember an occasion – it was in the torrid month of April in northern India – when I had been trying for the best part of a whole morning to locate the nest and young of a Black-bellied Finch-Lark in a parched, shingly riverbed. After what seemed an endless vigil, binoculars glued to my eyes, the male bird, insect in bill, who had been flitting about evasively from stone to stone in the vicinity, showed signs of getting over his nervousness. It looked as if at last he was about to visit the hidden nest. Just at this instant an individual, who had apparently been snooping on me from a distance, burst in on the scene noisily crunching the gravel under his hob-nails, and with gushing friendliness enquired if that was a telephone I was using and who I was trying to call up! Now, ornithologists are, as a rule, mild and harmless individuals, but that unknown one *will*, I am afraid, never cease to testify that they are prone to break out into inexplicable fits of unprovoked violence.

Most of us enjoy looking at beautiful birds and hearing their sweet songs. Yet how few there are who can name a bird when they see it, or recognise the songster in his song. And rarer still are those who can tell you anything about the life and habits of even our commonest species. The difficulty about recognising Indian birds and taking an intelligent interest in their ways of life has been, to a great extent, the absence of simple books with coloured pictures. This difficulty has happily been largely removed within recent years by several good publications like Whistler's *Popular Handbook of Indian Birds* and the more profusely illustrated

Book of Indian Birds brought out by the Bombay Natural History Society last year. So now no one need complain on this score at any rate.

There is an indefinable pleasure in meeting in the flesh a bird that one has seen in a picture or read about in a book, or heard of in legend or poetry. There is greater satisfaction in running to earth the builder of a strange nest that you happen to have come across on your rambles, or in shadowing and finally discovering the producer of a song you have heard. The pleasure is greater when you can discover some peculiarity in the habits of a bird: What it eats and how it procures its food; its behaviour towards enemies, towards others of its kind, and towards its young; how it reacts to danger or adapts itself to changed natural conditions, and so on.

All this is what makes bird watching a pursuit for the out of doors that is without rival. It can be indulged in by everybody with pleasure and profit. You don't need to be a trained zoologist to enjoy birds. Observations of people who watch birds intelligently, even though merely for pleasure, can be of great value to the scientist trying to unravel some knotty problem of animal behaviour in his laboratory. Indeed, frequently such observations, made from a fresh and perfectly unbiased angle, provide a clue which leads to the solution of the difficulty.

The bird population of every locality – even of a modest-sized city garden – is constantly changing. We all know that many of the species that are commonly seen during the winter months, say between October and March, are absent during the rest of the year. If one watches birds carefully enough from day to day and from week to week, the changes in the quantity and quality of the bird life become very evident. If you note down the times when a certain bird is first seen in a garden, and when last, over a number of years, you discover that there is a marked regularity in its comings and goings, and can usually foretell its movements fairly accurately. Just as there is this yearly rhythm or cycle – most clearly seen in the migrations of birds and in their nesting seasons – so there are other rhythms of more frequent occurrence connected with temperature, rainfall, vegetation, insect life, and so on which the regular birdwatcher is able to record.

Now, these are things that cannot be done within the walls of a museum or learnt from the pages of a book. The museum worker studies details of the dead bird; he studies their relationships and sorts them out into groups; he neatly tags a label on to them and gives to each dry, shrivelled-up skin a mouthful of a Latin name. It cannot be denied that his job too is a very necessary one, for unless you know a bird precisely enough to be able to tie a proper label to it, it is difficult to study it in the field. But I feel that although a bird in the hand may sometimes be worth two in the bush, we have hitherto given far too much importance to the study of dead material in museums at the expense of the live bird in the field. It has been a fashion in scientific circles – but one I am glad to say which is fast changing – to look askance at field naturalists as being merely amateurs and dabbling in "bird lore" which need not be taken too seriously. The error of this view has been demonstrated again and again, and is now coming to be realised.

However, all this is perhaps beside the point. The object of these talks is really to interest listeners, in the first instance for the healthy pleasure and satisfaction bird watching affords rather than for its intrinsic scientific possibilities. I shall recount an experience.

A few years ago I had a building colony of Baya Weaver-birds under close and regular observation for several months running. To get on a level with the babool tree on which the nests hung, I had rigged up a raised platform on which I spent several hours each day with camera, binoculars, and notebook concealed behind a screen of leaves and branches. In a short time the birds became perfectly accustomed to this weird contraption almost in their midst. They worked at their ease and paid not the slightest attention to me, perched only a few feet away, even when from time to time there were mysterious clattering sounds from within as the Reflex shutter was released and the slides changed. I remember this particular occasion because of a question it forcibly thrust on my mind – the question as to whether birds possess a Conscience, and what is in reality the thing that we call Conscience. I noted down the various incidents almost as they occurred.

While the owner of a half-built nest was away with a party of fellow-builders to procure fresh grass strips from a field of young paddy plants close by, I observed his neighbour, who had stayed behind, surreptitiously hop across to the unattended nest and tug feverishly at two or three of the interwoven strands. Presently he flew off with the booty to his own structure and proceeded to work them into the fabric of his own nest. I soon discovered that this was the only laggard in this industrious colony. He seldom flew out with the others to get his own nesting material, and he was in fact, an habitual offender. Whether it was the Little Inner Voice, or whether it was the memory of some unsavoury past experience I cannot tell, but the pilfering bird certainly showed every evidence of guilt and sheepishness in his actions. His hurried pulls, his furtive glances around, and his hasty departure before the return of the "supply column" all evinced plainly that the bird was fully aware that what it was doing is *Not Done.* When making our customs declarations, for instance, is it fear of consequences if caught out, or is it – as we smugly imagine – a Righteous Conscience that guides our pen?

I was eye-witness to this pilferer's shady practices again and again. It was also clear to me that the rightful owner never ceased to suspect his neighbour. He had not failed to mark on his return that his nest had been mauled about. More than once I had seen him cast accusing glances at his neighbour who continued to work on in pretended innocence and complacency. He must surely also have noticed that the material the suspect was using was browned by exposure, and not fresh and green like that procured directly from the fields. But although the circumstantial evidence was perhaps damning enough to convict No. 2 in a court of law, the injured party took no action beyond looking distinctly aggrieved. Only on one occasion, soon after, when he returned rather unexpectedly to the scene and caught the robber red-handed, was there plying of bills and flying of feathers while the culprit screamed blue murder and fluttered piteously.

My joy and satisfaction were undisguised. No. 2's "Conscience" had had a rude awakening, and for the rest of my vigil that day, he behaved with the utmost respectability.

2

Further Experiences in Bird Watching*

As I have already introduced, in my first talk on bird watching, the colony of Weaver-birds I once had under prolonged observation, it seems satisfactory to pursue the theme and to describe some more of my experiences during this investigation. It is not often that one gets an opportunity like that for continued and intensive watching over a sufficiently long period to enable one to become really intimate with one's subject. Personally I have seldom got so much pleasure and satisfaction as from those hundred-odd hours that I spent within my hide.

The nest colony was located on a babool tree standing in the centre of a small tank which at this time of year had become a vast expanse of open water about thigh-deep. The machan was a crude step-ladder-like contraption on which I could perch on a stool in comparative comfort, concealed behind a screen of leafy branches all round. This position was raised enough to bring me up more or less on a level with the nests. For photography and prolonged watching this is an important and very necessary detail if you don't happen to be born with a neck of India-rubber.

*14 March 1942, Bombay.

Every morning, sometimes with a break of a day or two in between, I got into the hide at about 8 armed with camera, binoculars, and notebook, and stayed there between 1½ and 4 hours at a time. What struck me particularly as rather unusual after a very short time of watching was that there were many more completed nests in this colony than there were birds building, and that almost all the builders were cocks in their dapper breeding attire of golden yellow and dark brown. All the accounts of the Baya that I had previously seen in books agree – it is more than likely the same account had been copied from book to book – that the male and female worked jointly in the building of the nest, so I had started my watching more or less with this preconceived notion. Now it soon became obvious that local bayas had not consulted the books, for if the books were correct, where were the hens? Day after day I watched the cocks busily working away but there was no sign as yet of any hens! The few that were present on the colony were in occupation of the completed nests, evidently on eggs. I only got momentary glimpses of them as they came and went. Who were the cocks building for? Where were the hens keeping? Would they turn up later? I was getting intrigued. One morning, a few days later, I suddenly perceived that a party of hens had made their appearance on the nest tree. This was the occasion for much unprecedented excitement and noise among the builders. The cocks left their work; there was a great deal of impetuous strutting, posturing, and showing off before the hens – a demonstration which seemed to leave the ladies cold. They remained perfectly indifferent and unresponsive, and often fled from the tree altogether to avoid the gushing advances. They returned soon, however, and amidst all this amorous bustle they kept hopping about the branches rather meaninglessly, as it seemed at first, but their purpose soon became apparent. The initial outburst of excitement having abated, the cocks gradually resumed their building activities. Now I observed that the hens had become bolder. They hopped about from one half-built nest to another as if deliberately inspecting them. One would perch on the outside of a nest for a while, and then go on to the cross bar under the dome to view the interior. While this was taking place the excitement of the particular owner and builder concerned was ludicrous to behold. It reminded me forcibly of a certain scene of aggressive love-making in that immortal comedy *Charley's Aunt*. The upshot of all these happenings was that some of the nests were approved by these roving females who, without further ceremony, proceeded to appropriate them and to establish themselves in possession. It frequently happened that the choice of two hens fell upon the same "Desirable Residence". Much unladylike conduct and language ensued. Bills plied viciously and feathers flew – until one of them decided to withdraw. From now on the victorious female and the builder of the nest become wife and husband. For the next few days they are inseparable, working harmoniously together. He flying out now and again to fetch fresh paddy leaf strips and doing the lion's share of the work, she mostly occupied with putting the egg-chamber into shape – sometimes lining it with a feather – and looking after what we may call interior decoration. After the nest is completed and she has laid her eggs and commenced brooding them, I wonder within myself what the cock is going to do next since he does not seem deeply interested in his menage any longer. I presently discover that the cock has commenced building another nest nearby and is now working away at it with gusto. In about a week's time when this nest – No. 2 – has reached a sufficiently advanced state, I find that there is again a female visitation soon after and I observe him with another lady friend helping him in his task. Her advent has been accompanied by the same excitement, fluttering, chasing and singing as marked the acquisition of wife No. 1. Soon after, the pair complete this second nest and this hen is also fairly on the way to bringing up a family. The cock continues on giving finishing touches to this nest and elongating the entrance tube for a time, reinforcing the suspension so as to withstand the buffeting from strong monsoon gales with the added weight of the family to come and so on. But very soon I see him beginning on a 3rd nest which in due course is appropriated by a 3rd female; and sometimes a fourth is similarly accommodated. It is noticeable that some nests fail to progress beyond the half-built stage – i.e. the stage at which they are normally annexed by a roving female. Such nests, evidently, are the ones that – due to some defect in construction perceptible only to the capricious female eye – have not been approved.

I have been able to watch that not only are such unapproved nests deserted by their builders, who promptly try again by starting on another, but that while working on their new structures these cocks often deliberately hop across to them and work with obvious will and purpose to demolish them by biting off the suspension. I believe that the incomplete nests one commonly sees littering the ground under every Baya colony are such derelicts. Of course it sometimes also happens that a completed nest with eggs already laid in it is found jettisoned. This is probably the criminal act of some disgruntled member of the colony.

One of the myths that have been bequeathed to us by old writers is that after a pair of Baya have completed a nest and the hen is settled on eggs, the cock proceeds to build himself another solely for his own enjoyment and benefit – to rest and swing by day and to sleep in at night, we are told. The male is said never to complete this nest on purpose but to leave it at a halfway stage. I am afraid that this proves to be just fanciful imagining.

The half-built nests commonly seen in a nesting colony – termed cock nests – are in reality nothing other than ones that have failed to attract female tenants. As a matter of fact, after they have finished the day's work the cocks do not sleep in the colony at all. Soon after sunset they leave the hens in the nests and repair long distances to a communal roost or chummery in some reedbed or mangrove swamp. Thus the question of their using the so-called cock nests for sleeping in at night does not arise. Most of you have no doubt heard another more poetic myth concerning the Baya – the one about its employing fireflies to light up its abode at night. It is a pretty tale and it seems iconoclastic to destroy it. We are told that Bayas catch fireflies and stick them in the blob of mud found in nearly every Baya nest. To do this the fireflies must be pressed in while the mud is wet. If so, then all the fireflies must be killed either in the process or as soon as the mud dries. Now the unfortunate part is that dead fireflies do not emit any light. When they die, the illumination is naturally switched off, hence the Baya can derive no benefit from them as an aid to its reading in bed. So it is in fact total blackout inside.

The purpose of this blob of mud, by the way, is a mystery. It has been suggested that its weight may help to steady the freely swaying nest in a gale. Considering that the mud employed rarely weighs more than a couple of ounces, this explanation seems hardly satisfactory – some other must be looked for. This is a point that calls for further investigation.

3A

*Chand Hairat Parandon aur Janwaron ke Ghar: Chand Bare aur Chhote Ghonsla Bananewale**

PARANDON KI EK *bari khasiat hai keh unmen se aksar kisi na kisi tarah ke ghonsle banate hain jin men unke undey diay jate hain aur unke bachchon ki paidaish aur parvarish hoti hai. Albat yeh bat kai aur janwaron men bhi paee jati hai. Chunancheh chand qism ki machhli aur chand chau payay bhi apne liay ghonsle taiyar kar lete hain.*

Parandon ke ghonsle tarah tarah ke hote hain. Koee to aise ke jisme kisi khas karigari ya hoshiari nahin paee jati. Sub se simple *ghonsle woh jo zamin par banaye jate hain. Is ka bananewala zamin par sirf ek chhota sa garha kured leta hai, aur is may apne unday de deta hai. Un par kuchh din baith kar un men se bachchey nikalta hai. Ba'az waqt is piala-numa garha men ghas ke tinke jama kar leta hai, takeh undey goya ek narm bistar par rahain. Zamin par rehne aur daorne wale parande, masalan* Africa *ka shutr-murgh aur hamare mulk ki titori, waghaira, is quism ke ghonsle banate hain.*

Ba'az parandon ke ghonsle nanayat nafees aur hairat angez hote hain. Insan hairan reh jata hai keh woh aisi ajib o gharib imarat

*School Broadcast, 9 October 1946, Bombay.

taiyaar karna kahan aur kis tarah seekhey. Parandon ki dimaghi haisiat ko dekhte hooay kaha ja sakta hai ke un men ziada soch bichar karneka maada nahin. Agar cheh chand qismen aise ghosle banati hain jis men ghliban bohat dimaghi tezi aur hoshiari ki zaroorat chahiay, lekin zahir hai keh dar asal yeh chalaki sirf paon aur chonch ki hai, aur dimagh ki nahin.

Har qism ka paranda usi tarah ka ghonsla bana sakta aur banata hai jis may ke woh khud paida huwa tha. Aur yeh hunar woh apne sath goya unday men se hi lekar nikalta hai; man bap ke sikhane ka natija nahin. Is bat ki sachchaee ka tajurba asani se kia ja sakta hai. Dekhne me ata hai keh agar masalan Baya ke bachchey ghonsle se nikal liay jaen, aur unke pinjray me is tarah parvarish ki jae ke unki qism ke aur parandon se unka milna julna aur wasta mutlaq na rahe, taham jab unka ghonsla bananeka mausam aiga, woh usi tarah ka ghonsla taiyar karenge jaise men woh khud paida huay thay. Is halat ka poori taor se samajhna hamare liay asan nahin, lekin behar hal is se yeh to zahir hai ke ghonsla bananeka maada parandon men khud ba khud maojood hai, aur yeh hunar man bap se sikha huwa nahin.

Isi tarah jo parandey sardi aur barf se bachne ke liye jaron ke maosam men garm mulkon ko chal baste hain, woh bhi bin seekhe aur bin samjhe chale jate hain. Bachchpane ka ba'ad pahle hi safar par unko na to yeh khabar ho sakti hai ke woh kahan ja rahe hain, na toh yeh ke kisleeay ja rahe hain, na kitne sao mile chalna hoga, nay yeh akharkar kahan pohchenge. Aisa samjha jata hai ke jo parandon men bariki se sochne ka maada nahin, taham koiee aisi cheez ki madad say unka kam chal jata hai jaise masalan hamen jab koee marne ke liay hath uthata hai to ham bekhood apni ankh band kar lete hain. Yeh barkat soche ba'ad nahin ki jati, balke aise maoqon par khud ba khud ho hi jati hai.

Hamare mulk ka Baya ek aisa paranda hai jise har shakhs janta hoga. Khwah parande ko sirf nam se hi, lekin aisa koee bachcha ya boorha mushkil se milega jisne kabhi na kabhi Baya ka hooka-numa ya botal-numa jhonj na dekha ho. Yeh ghosle daihati ilaqon men nahayat kasrat se babool aur aur darakhton par tange hooey nazar atay hain. Agarcheh ek isqadar aam cheez hai, lekin Baya ka ghonsla Hindustan ke parandon ka ek sab se hairat-angez karigari ka namoona hai. Go ke uska me'mar ek chhoti si chiria hai lekin ghonsla is safai, hunarmandi aur mazbooti say buna hua hota hai ki poori taqat se bhi mushkil se hi use tor sakte hain. Uske bunne men oomooman dhan ki ghas istemal ki jati hai, aur isi taran ki aur ghas jiski kinar par manin dant hote hain, jaise lakri katne ka aara. Yeh dant aise hain ke agar aap uspar apni oongly chalaven to sirf ek hi tarf chal sakegi. Doosri tarf chalanen men danton se rukawat mahsoos hovegi aur tezi ki wajeh se oongly cut javegi. Jab Baya is ghas ka ek tinka apne ghosle men bunta hai to usay sirf ek hi tarf khainch sakta hai. Jab kafi mazbooti se tinke ko ek dafa under tan chukta hai to yeh dant aptne lagte bilagte tinkon ko aisa jakar lete hain ke sari bunat tani hooee hi rahti hai. Baya in chhoti chhoti cheezon ka is khoobi se faida leta hai, ke waqi yeh manna dushwar hai ke sara kam bin samjhe soche kia jata hai, goya ek machine chal rahi ho.

Baya ke hairat angez jhonj ka zikr karte huey, yeh zaroor hai ke uski ajeeb o gharib nesting habits *par bhi chand alfaz kahe javen. Thore sal huey ke mujhe khudko zati taor par is baat ki chhan been karneka ek maoqa pesh hua tha. Is daor me chand cheezon ka pakki taor se pata chala jin par peshtar bohat* (uncertainty) *thi.*

Mere tajrube se yeh zahir hua ke Baya men ghonsla sirf nar hi banata hai aur is kam me madin ka bohat kam dakhal hai. Jab unday bachchay ka maosam ata hai – yane barsat ka, jis waqt ghonsle ke liay maozoon ghas mohayya ho sakti hai – to chand nar ekhatta ho kar kisi babool ya khajoor par apni apni teni pasand kar ke ghonsla bananeka kam shuroo' kar dete hain. Is waqt, or is ke ba'ad kai dinon tak yahan madinon ka nam o nishan bhi nahin hota. Sirf jab jhonj adha, ya kuchh ziada, taiyar ho chukta hai oosi waqt madinan pehli martaba is nao abadi men namoodar hoti hain. Aate hi woh faoran ek se doosre jhonj par koodti phirti nazar aati hain, aur is silsile men ghonsle ke ander bhi dakhil hoti hain. Zahiran unka mansha yeh hai ke me'mar ka kam poori taor say inspect *karen. Agar koee madin ko koee jhonj khatir khwah ma'loom hua aur pasand aa gaya to woh faoran uspe apna qabza jama leti hai. Goya yeh ek tariqa hai nar ko zahir karne ka ke woh usay shaohar qabul karti hai. Ab se aage chal kar mia bibi milkar apna ghonsla taiyar kar dete hain, agarcheh madin ka kam ziadatar ander ke hissay men hi hota hai. Is ke jald hi ba'ad unday diay jate hain, aur madin unpar baith jati hai. Nar ka kam maosam ke lehaz se abtak khatam nahin hua. Woh apne pehle jhonj ke qarib men aur ek tehni pasand kar kar, ek doosra ghar banana shuroo' kar deta hai, jiska aage chalkar pahle sa hi hal hota hai. Ek doosri madin is ghonsle me bhi basera kar leti hai. Is taor se, ek hi maosam men, ek khush kismet shaohar ko do, teen ya char biwian naseeb ho jati hain aur dus ya bara bachchay.*

Hindustan ke parandon men bohat se aur bhi hain jink ke ghonsle isi tarah hairat angez aur qabil-e-nazar hain. Waqt ki tangi hone se auron ka bian aaj tafsil se nahin kia ja sakta. Aap logon ne Dirzee ya Tailor Bird *ka shohra to zaroor suna hi hoga. Yeh ek nanhi si chiria hai jo aam taor par hamare baghon me paee jati hai, agarcheh ziada ta'dad men nahin. Har bagh jahan kisi hi qism ke jhar ya powde hon wahan ek ya do joray zaroor maojood hote hain. Yeh chiria apne ghonsle ke liay do ya teen bare ugte huay patton ko see kar ek bhoongli si taiyar kar leti hai. Apni chonch se sooi ka kam lekar is nafasat aur mazbooti say silai karti hai ke khud aur khudke bachchon ka wazn, aur barishi hawa ke toofani jhonke usey kuchch nuqsan nahin pohoncha sakte.*

Hamare parandon men har qism ke karigar maojood hain. Aaplogon ke samne julaha aur darzi pesh kar chukka hoon. Leejiay ab ek raj ya kariay ka hal sunye.

Aap men se aksar ghaliban Flamingo *se to waqifat rakhte honge. Rani ke bagheeche men jo pani ke parandon ka pinjra hai wahan yeh paranda har waqt dekha ja sakta hai. Isay Hindustani men Raj-hans aur aur namon se pukarte hain. Kutch riasat men – jahan ke barsati maosam me beshumar ta'dad me paya jata hai – isay Hanj kehte hain. Yeh ek bara aur ajeeb o ghareeb janwar hai. Lambi patli si tangen, lambi samp jaisi gardan, aur moti si bhaddi, muri hooi lal chonch. In ke alawa uske sufed par surkhi aur gulabi ma'il hote hain aur yeh sab milkar uska dikhao aisa nirala keh uski pehchan me kisi qism ka dhoka ya ghalti nahin ho sakti. Hindustan me hame aaj tak ek hi jaga ma'loom hai jahan yeh paranda apne ghonsle banata hai. Yeh wohi reteela maidan jo Sind aur Kutch ke darmian hai aur jise Rann kehte hain. Is zamin par barsaat ke aakhari dinon men chhitla sa pani jama' rehta hai. Is maosam men yahan ghaliban poore Hindustan ke Flamingo ekhatta ho jate hain aur apne ghonsle banakar unday bachchey dete hain. Flamingo ka ghonsla ek mutti ka tela hota hai, jo oonchai men 1½ ya 2 foot tak hota hai, aur dakhne men gonde ki topi se kuchh kuchh mushabehat rakhta hai. Paranda apni chonch se keechar ekhatta kar kar oosi taor se yeh tela taiyyar karta hai jaisa ke ek raj choona* cement *aur apne* trowel *se kare. Aap logon ko khial hoga keh jab karia apna masala taiyyar karta hai to pahle uska ek tela sa bana leta hai jiske tonch par ek chhitla garha pani ke liay rakhta hai ta keh masala sookh na jane pawe.* Flamingo *ke ghonsle bhi isi tarah ke banaye jate hain, aur dhoop ki tez garmi se bohat jald pathar jaise sakht ho jate hain. Oopar ke garhe me ek unda dia jata hai. Yeh ghonsla nehayat kasrat se kihichakhhich banaye jate hain, aur isi tarah jaisa ek shahr me insanon ka ghar. Chunancheh ghonsle ki jaga ko* Famingo *ka shahr kaha jata hai. Pichle dinon me mujhe ek aisay shahr ke tajruba hooa tha jahan andazan do lakh se ziada ghonsle honge. Jab har ghonsla par uska malik unday par baitha hoowa hota hai to door se ek nehayat ajeeb o ghareeb manzar dekhai deta hai, goya ek sufed aur gulabi phoolonka maidan.*

3B

Some Amazing Homes of Birds and Animals*

THE SPECIALITY OF birds is that they make nests of one kind or another in which they lay their eggs and bring up their young. However, there are certain types of fish and some four-legged animals that also make nests for themselves.

Birds' nests are of many different types. The simplest ones that do not need much expertise or skill are just a small shallow bowl made on the ground by the bird by scraping the soil. Tufts of grass are gathered and placed to make a soft bed on which eggs may be safely laid. The young chicks emerge after the bird has sat for some days on these eggs. Birds that live and run on the ground, such as the ostrich in Africa and the lapwing in our country, make this kind of nest.

Most birds' nests are very sophisticated and quite amazing. People have long wondered how they learnt to build these unusual homes! It is said that birds do not have the ability to think because their brains do not have the capacity for thought. However, many kinds of nests give us the impression that much brainwork and ingenuity is needed to make them – but of course it is evident that this is the skill of the birds' feet and beaks, not their brains.

*Translation of 3A above. School Broadcast, 9 October 1946, Bombay.

Each kind of bird makes – and can only make – the type of nest it was born in. This talent is therefore inherent in a bird from the time of its birth and is not learned from its parents. It is easy to demonstrate the truth of this. For instance, if Baya chicks are removed from their nest and reared in a cage where they have absolutely no interaction with birds of their own kind, it has been found that when the nesting season comes, they make the same type of nest as the one in which they were born. This instinct is not really easy for us to understand, but the clear conclusion is that the technique of nest-making is innate in birds and not a learnt art.

In the same way, certain birds that migrate to warm countries in winter to escape from snow and cold, go off with no thought or understanding of what they are doing. When their young ones grow up and set out on their very first migration flight, they too have no idea where they are headed, why they are going there, how many hundreds of miles they must go, or where they will reach at last. The journey is not thought out by the bird, but happens naturally when the time comes. Since birds lack the capacity for detailed thought, we must infer that there is something else that helps them to act as they do – as, for instance, if a hand is raised against us, we instinctively flinch and close our eyes.

Our country's Baya is a bird that everyone is likely to know, at least by sight if not by name. Is there any child or adult who has never seen the Baya's hookah-shaped or bottle-shaped nest? Many of these can be found hanging from babool and other trees in the countryside. Though the Baya is quite common, its nest is the finest example of craftsmanship among all the birds in Hindustan. This small bird weaves its nest so tightly, so neatly, and with such skill that it cannot be broken or torn by human hands, no matter how much force is used!

Paddy leaves, and the leaves of other similar grasses that are edged with "teeth" – like those of a wood-cutting saw – are the materials used for weaving. The "teeth" on the long leaves are all in one direction, so, though you can run your finger along the edge in the same direction without injury, if you move it the opposite way they are so sharp as to cut your finger.

When the Baya takes a blade of this kind of grass to weave its nest, it can pull only in one direction. Once the grass strip has been pulled tight in the nest, it attaches itself with its "teeth" to the adjoining blades of grass to become a firmly woven structure. The way the Baya is cleverly able to use these small resources makes it all the more difficult for us to believe that it does so with no thought or understanding, but almost mechanically.

While speaking of Bayas, it is necessary to say a few words about their interesting nesting habits. For several years I have had the opportunity to study them in some detail, during which time various aspects of their lives which were mysterious became clear. From my experience, it became obvious that only the male Baya builds nests, and that in this work the female has very little to do. With the onset of their breeding season, that is, during the rains, at which time suitable grasses are abundant, several males get together and start building nests on babool or date-palm trees, selecting the branches that seem the choicest. During this time, and for many days after, there is no sign of the females. Only when the nests are half complete, or a bit more, do the females arrive for the first time to see these newly built homes. As soon as they come, they start hopping from one nest to the next and can be seen entering some of them. It appears that they intend to carefully inspect the work of the architect. When a female likes one of the nests, or at any rate finds it satisfactory, she straightaway takes possession of it. It is her way of showing that she accepts the builder of that particular nest as her mate. From then on, husband and wife together complete the nest, usually with the female working on the interior. Soon afterwards, eggs are laid and the female sits on them.

The male's work for the season is not yet finished, for he chooses a nearby branch and starts building another nest near his old one. Again, as before, in due course a second female establishes herself in this nest too. By this means the lucky male gets two, three or even four wives in one season and about ten or twelve babies.

There are many more birds in Hindustan that make all kinds of wonderful and unusual nests. Time being short, it is not possible to describe them all today. You will certainly have heard the well-known call of the Tailor Bird. This is a tiny bird usually found in our gardens, though not in large numbers. One or two pairs are sure to be seen in gardens with different kinds of bushes and plants. To make their nests, these birds use their sharp beaks to stitch together two or three large leaves growing on a single plant to create something like a pouch. The nest is strong enough to bear the weight of the bird's own body as well as of its babies and to not be harmed by rain, wind, or storm.

Our birds have many kinds of skills. I have presented to you the weaver and the tailor. Come now, to hear about a mason.

The Flamingo must be familiar to most of you. It can be seen at any time in the waterbirds enclosure in Rani Baug. In Hindustani this bird is called *Raj-hans*, as well as by other names. In the district of Kutch, where it is found in huge numbers during the rainy season, it is called *Hanj*. This is a large and curious-looking creature with tall thin legs, long snake-like neck, stout body, and a curved red beak. Apart from these, and its white-and-pink feathers, its appearance is so unique that there can be no mistake or confusion in recognising it. There is only one location in Hindustan where this bird builds its nest, this being the sandy expanse between Sind and Kutch called the Rann. During the last days of the monsoon, a layer of water remains accumulated on the ground in the area. Almost all the flamingos in the country gather together at this time to build their nests and lay their eggs for hatching.

A Flamingo nest is like a raised mound of mud, about 1½ feet to 2 feet high, which looks somewhat like a tall cap. The bird goes on collecting slushy mud in its beak and builds the mound exactly as a mason uses his trowel when plastering lime and cement.

All of you will know that when a construction worker prepares the cement mixture, he makes a kind of mound, on the surface of which he pours water to prevent it from drying. Flamingo nests are made in the same way, and under the blazing heat of the sun they soon become hard as stone.

A single egg is laid within the small cup-like depression at the top. These nests are built closely packed together, almost like our houses in a city; therefore the place is referred to as Flamingo City. Some days ago I heard of such a city with perhaps as many as two lakh nests. When each of the nests has a bird sitting on it, the sight is extraordinary – like a field of white and pink flowers.

4

Bird Watching*

If I am asked why I spend hours and days in watching birds when I might be doing something more useful, I must admit that I do not always find it easy to produce a convincing reply on the spur of the moment. Yet, on reflection, I see no difficulty in putting up half a dozen good reasons why I do so. But I suspect that with most enquirers the crux of the question is that one word – "useful". If by useful they mean ability to produce cash dividends, then it is well not to try to justify bird watching. For there is perhaps no other occupation less likely to offer a livelihood than the study of birds, particularly in India where its importance is as yet so little realised. Thus it is not altogether surprising that, to the man in the street or in the shop or on the share bazaar, watching birds should seem a completely daft undertaking. Even in countries more advanced than ours, bird study as a profession offers extremely limited possibilities, and those not very lucrative. In India such openings are non-existent. Studying birds as a hobby, however, is not the same thing as adopting it for a profession. The dividends it pays are of the spirit only.

It is perhaps true that bird watching has been, and to some extent still is, confined more or less to the class of persons known

*8 January 1952, Bombay.

to the industrious poor as the idle rich. The reason for this is not difficult to see, but with the growing realisation of the aesthetic and cultural value of nature study, and the importance attached to it in most progressive countries as a training for the young, the "class barrier" is fast disappearing. The common man is beginning to discover the joy and fascination of the out-of-doors, and the satisfaction to be derived from an intimacy with wild creatures in their native setting, the spiritual elation it produces, and the breadth it imparts to his outlook. I have largely had the opportunity of visiting a number of countries in Europe and was astounded by the keen and almost universal interest taken in bird study by every stratum of the populace, of all ages and both sexes. Particularly so is this the case in England and the Scandinavian countries of Denmark and Sweden. The keenness and knowledgeability of many of the young people I met concerning their local bird fauna was truly amazing, and their output of really high-class field work is naturally large. Of the type of so-called amateur birdwatchers who are making valuable contributions to science I would cite as example a young barber's assistant in Basel who works under the direction of a university professor. This young man is engaged on a problem connected with the population dynamics of different species of titmouse, and has already collected some exceedingly valuable and intricate data. He crops his customers' hair all week long and waits impatiently for the clock to strike one on Saturday afternoons. Immediately the shop is shut, he jumps on his bicycle with his binoculars and his rucksack (containing his nest marking rings, weighing scales, and other paraphernalia) and makes a beeline for the forest four miles away which is the scene of his operations. He plunges into the investigation the rest of Saturday and all Sunday and is back again to attack his customers' heads and beards betimes on Monday morning!

Till not so long ago, bird watching was regarded by scientific highbrows and professional museum men as a harmless enough but somewhat childish way of killing time. The observations of field naturalists were sometimes treated with condescending tolerance, but little scientific importance was conceded to them. This gave some people the idea that because they do not kill and stuff birds and preserve their dry skins, they were incapable of contributing anything seriously worthwhile to the study of birds. It is a fundamental truth that before one can begin to learn about anything one must be able to recognise it and give it a name. That is why all zoological work has to commence with collection and classification of specimens. Specimens have enabled scientists to arrange our birds into different families and to describe the characters by which one species may be distinguished from another. But even here in India, bird study has now reached a stage when it is unnecessary – except in special localities and by specialists who know what to look for – to go on collecting bird skins in a haphazard manner any longer. The gun and the skinning knife must now give way to the binoculars, the camera, and the notebook. Our greatest need today is to learn facts about the living bird, its food and habitat preferences, its breeding habits and courtship ceremonies, its social life, emotions, behaviour, adaptations, and so on. These are not things that can be studied in a musty museum from dry and shrivelled-up skins with the help of callipers and slide rules. They are things that people like you and me who watch living birds intelligently enough to enjoy them can contribute to, as we wander about the fields and forests in the open air and under the blue sky. All you need in the way of equipment is a good pair of field glasses, a notebook and pencil, a goodly stock of patience, and the capacity to observe keenly and record faithfully. That is the sort of study which we sorely need in India today and for which we must get recruits and more recruits in every part of the country.

Recognising a bird in the field is not the end of bird study; it is just the beginning, and merely a means to the end. Since the positive determination of a species is quite essential for any notes concerning it to be of scientific value, it behoves observers to exercise scrupulous care. Many a useful observation is ruined by faulty or doubtful identification, and once a mistake finds its way into published literature it is seldom possible to correct it effectively, or to repair its author's reputation.

Bird watching is a fascinating outdoor game, and everyone who wishes to extract the fullest enjoyment from it and to contribute to scientific knowledge must first learn to play it. As with every game of skill, patience and perseverance are essential in the early stages. But proficiency is quickly acquired and it snowballs with practice at an amazing rate. With detailed notes jotted down in the field and sufficient persistence to follow, it is usually not difficult to run to earth even an uncommon species with the help of bird books or museum specimens. Some very excellent books are now obtainable in England and America – also in other European countries – specially designed to help the amateur by means of ingeniously devised simple keys and sketches. Roger Tory Peterson's *A Field Guide to the Birds* and James Fisher's *Bird Recognition* in the Pelican series (of which as far as I know only the first volume, *Wading Birds*, has so far appeared) are commendable models. Unfortunately we have nothing in the same class available for Indian birds, though Whistler's *Popular Handbook of Indian Birds* has in my opinion tried to provide what a former generation lacked, and is helpful to the beginner up to a point.

The royal road to learning bird identification is of course to be out in the field with one who, even though not expert, is in the habit of watching birds and familiar at least with the common species of his neighbourhood. Familiarity with common local birds is a great advantage because once you have acquired that basic knowledge it is much easier to spot the uncommon. You now also possess same standards of size, length of bill, tail, neck, legs, and so on for making comparisons.

Upon meeting a strange bird it is good to take down as detailed notes as possible on the spot and while you are observing the bird. Size, colour, pattern, and comparative lengths of the different parts, whether crested or not, colour of eyes, bill, legs, and any other unfeathered portions and notes of that sort, are most helpful. The more detailed and accurate your notes are, the greater your chances of correct identification later. Leave nothing to memory. Memory is a thoroughly unreliable jade and delights in playing the most fantastic tricks to lead you astray. Strange as it may sound, it is nevertheless true that, after one has reached a certain stage of proficiency in bird recognition, one begins to depend less and less on colours as the leading clue except only in a very general way. The thing that now looms large in importance is an undefinable sum total of the way, maybe, a bird carries its neck and body, turns its head or flicks its tail, flits from bush to bush, or moves on the ground. A combination of all these points with the overall proportions of the wings to tail to legs and so on has come to be known to British bird students as "jizz". I don't know who invented this word, but it has now come to mean just what ornithologists wish it to express. Therefore, with growing practice in field work the birdwatcher comes to depend more and more on "jizz" for identifying a bird rather than on the actual details of colouring. Once you have familiarised yourself with the "jizz" of a particular group of birds – say the flycatchers – it is usually a comparatively simple matter to arrive at your species; or at any rate to narrow down the field of possibilities to within workable proportions.

Personally, I consider it almost as important to note the environment in which a bird is seen, and also its preoccupation at the time, since these clues narrow down the range of possibilities still further. To take an example. A bird is described to you as black and slightly larger than a Jungle Crow, and with a pointed bill. If you are told at the same time that several such birds were sitting on a dead tree in the middle of a tank sunning themselves with wings stretched out and open, you are almost certain that it cannot be any species of crow. If you further learn that the bird flew down and alighted on the water, you are left in no doubt whatsoever that the bird was a cormorant.

Unfortunately no bird book will be able to convey to you with any degree of adequacy the song or call of a bird. This is simply because it is impossible to devise a satisfactory system of expressing bird calls in print. Nothing short of a gramophone record can give a proper idea. And considering that there are no recordings so far available for Indian birds, the only alternative is to familiarise yourself with calls and songs in the field and note them down in your own way. They may, with practice, become useful to yourself even if not to others.

5

Birding in Sikkim*

AN ORNITHOLOGICAL expedition to Sikkim, sponsored by the Bombay Natural History Society under my leadership and made possible through the sympathetic enthusiasm of one of the Society's vice-patrons, Mr W.T. Loke of Singapore, has just returned after a successful three months' work in the field. In the course of this talk and the next I shall try to introduce this fascinating strip of mountainous country to listeners, and to give some impressions of it as from a wandering student of birds. While on the genesis of the expedition I must also record with gratefulness the helpful co-operation it received from the Sikkim State government so vital for the success of a scientific enterprise in a thinly populated district where normal facilities are scarce and can usually be organised only through official channels.

To the exploring naturalist, interested in plants, birds, and butterflies, Sikkim has always been the land of hope and glory. It lies at the western extremity of the Eastern Himalayas and is an oblong wedge of mountain country about forty miles broad, west to east, by a hundred miles deep, north to south. It is roughly bounded by Tibet in the north, Nepal in the west, the

*20 March 1953, Bombay.

Darjeeling District of West Bengal in the south, and Bhutan in the east. On account of its natural position – nearness to the Bay of Bengal and direct exposure to the moisture-laden winds of the south-west monsoon – it is perhaps the most humid tract in the entire chain of the Himalayas. The section west of central Nepal is much less humid, a feature reflected directly in all its plant and animal life. An analysis on the races of typically Himalayan birds collected along the southern aspect of the entire Himalayan axis suggests that the zoogeographical boundary between the Eastern and Western Himalayas lies somewhere in the region of the Arun-Kosi river in eastern Nepal, about fifty miles west of the Sikkim border.

During the months from about May to October the monsoon is in full swing in Sikkim. The rainfall and humidity are so heavy that moving about the country is then impracticable. Beards of fungus sprout overnight on boots and scientific equipment, the sun remains more or less perpetually hidden, low clouds obscure the landscape, and zoological specimens collected are impossible to dry satisfactorily. Hordes of leeches secretly but incessantly sucking one's blood do not tend to lessen the general discomfort. Add to all this the frequent landslides which often remove gigantic chunks of the unstable mountains, along with perhaps the only foot track that leads across them, and the floods which follow the torrential downpours sweeping away the flimsy cane and bamboo bridges that precariously span the streams – and the picture of impracticability is complete. The monsoon, therefore, is a highly unsuitable season for an ornithological or any other kind of scientific field expedition. This is not to suggest that bird life is therefore any the less interesting at that time of year. Indeed, for some strange reason many humid forest birds choose the rainiest months for breeding, and we have as yet a great deal to learn about the nesting habits and particular ecology of these.

Under the circumstances it is only persons living on the spot, by making use of such fleeting opportunities as a temporary break in the weather may provide from time to time, who alone can supply the missing data. And this can come only when there is a more general intelligent interest in bird study and a greater number of resident observers scattered over the countryside. Since there are no signs of either at the moment, the data may be a long time coming.

The expedition commenced its work in November at an elevation of about 1200 ft in the Teesta Valley and gradually worked up to its highest collecting camp just under 12,000 ft in western Sikkim. A very good cross-section of the winter distribution of birds in the various altitudinal zones was thus obtained, and a considerable amount of data recorded concerning local migration, food, feeding habits, and general ecology of many uncommon species. For those unfamiliar with the word, it may be explained that "ecology" means the study of an organism in relation to its environment; in other words how the organism – in our case a particular species of bird – is adapted to live in its natural surroundings. Climate, vegetation, geology, and animal life of the bird's habitat all figure in a study of this kind. The bird is treated not as an independent entity but one which is intricately woven into the fabric of its environment, which in turn is influenced and moulded in some degree by the bird. Increasing importance is being given to ecology in the solution of biological problems, and it is obviously the only way in which the significance of the development and evolution of the different organisms can be properly understood.

For transport of its baggage and equipment the expedition used both mules and Sherpa porters. Sherpas have become almost legendary for their sturdiness and reliability, and successive Everest expeditions have employed these hardy and cheerful hillmen of Nepal for serious transport work over difficult country. A number of our porters were women. Sherpa women carry the same loads as men, namely one Bengal maund or about 80 lb. It was an object-lesson to see the effortless ease with which they literally romped up the steepest paths thus laden, or traversed a precipitous hillside with the agility of mountain goats even at the fag end of a gruelling day's march. Indeed it then came almost as a shock to our jaded he-man pride! These Sherpa dames were irrepressible in their mirth and jollity. On a halting day, the dak bungalow resounded with their fun and games to such a point that one was sometimes obliged to act the spoilsport and intervene. Happily enough such intervention never damped their ardour or produced sulks. Men and women removed themselves to a distance, usually not far enough, and the merrymaking was resumed as noisily as before.

Mule hire in Sikkim has recently rocketed to unheard-of heights. This is largely due to the enormous quantities of rice and building stores being transported into Tibet by the Chinese Government, mainly for troops stationed at the eastern border of Sikkim across the Nathu La, the main highway for Tibetan trade with India. On an exploratory visit in February 1952 we had paid Rs 5 per day as hire for a baggage mule. Now, nine months later, the hire demanded for the same jaded and overworked animal was Rs 8 – and latterly the Chinese were paying as much as Rs 15.

One of the major handicaps of touring in inner Sikkim is the paucity and lack of variety in local food supply. I am one of those who believe that an expedition should be as little encumbered with heavy stores as possible, and should manage to live chiefly off the land. Imported canned food is not only expensive, particularly when a largish party has to be kept fed for weeks and months, but tins are cumbersome to transport and put a quite disproportionately heavy strain on the budget, which for ornithological expeditions is seldom on liberal dimensions. In Sikkim local supplies are not only scarce but undependable. Vegetables, except potatoes sporadically, are unobtainable. The countryside is so thinly populated that eggs and milk are only available on rare occasions, and that in small quantities. During the first two or three days at each camp we would usually eat through the egg supply for miles around which obliged us to fall back once again on the inevitable dal and rice, assisted by boiled potatoes, when luck was in. If eggs are scarce and fitful, fowls are doubly so. It is difficult to understand why the locals do not grow more chickens. For apart from being good food for the owners in a country where good food is none too plentiful, fowls are always in demand and make their keeping well worth while. Full grown, tough old cocks, no longer good for breeding or any other useful purpose – all that the villagers would deign to sell us of their stock – were offered at Rs 6 to Rs 8 each.

The only item of food we found in abounding profusion, and cheaper than perhaps anywhere else in India today, was oranges. Sikkim oranges, though smaller than the Nagpur variety, are full of lusciousness and flavour. They grow best in the foothills up to about 3000 ft elevation and produce enormous crops. Long single files of coolies, almost staggering under huge pick-a-back baskets of oranges on their way to depots and railway outstation agencies, are a familiar sight on the hill paths during the winter months. Oranges that are Re 1 a hundred off the tree, snowball up to 6 or 8 annas a dozen by the time they reach the railhead at Siliguri, fifty or sixty miles away.

Although the natural delights and attractions of Sikkim as a playground for the trekker, mountaineer, and camera enthusiast are in no way inferior to Kashmir's, yet everything here is less organised and far more expensive. Therefore inspite of the numerous and well-appointed dak bungalows, Sikkim cannot at present be considered in terms of a cheap or even a particularly restful holiday. From the point of view of the naturalist and the mountaineer, however, this state of affairs is by no means to be deplored.

6

The Birds of Sikkim*

As a result of its heavy rainfall and great humidity, Sikkim is a land of luxurious vegetation. Its flora bears a close similarity with the rest of the Eastern Himalayas stretching to the extreme north-eastern frontier of India and beyond. It is also peculiarly akin to the plant life of the Malay Peninsula and Archipelago, many orders and families of plants typical of the Malayan region being significantly well represented here.

Three altitudinal zones of vegetation are roughly recognisable, though they have no clear-cut boundaries and merge quite gradually into one another. Allowing for considerable encroachments and recessions in these vegetational zones due to influences of physical configuration and other local causes not readily traceable, it may roughly be said that the normal tropical zone extends from the foothills to an altitude of about 4000 ft. It often contains deep, steep-sided valleys or gorges clothed in dense evergreen rain forest. Above this zone, and up to about 6500 ft, the country assumes a sub-tropical aspect. Beyond, and up to about 11,500 ft, comes the temperate zone which consists of a lower belt of non-coniferous trees up to 8000 ft or so, succeeded by an upper belt of conifers and rhododendrons. The larger rhododendron trees are draped thickly with foot-long beards of moss; thickets of dwarf

*20 March 1953, Bombay.

rhododendrons of innumerable species form the undergrowth towards the highest limits of this zone. When in full bloom in mid-May these shrubs present a magnificent blaze of colour such as must be seen to be believed. The Alpine zone stretches above the 12,000 ft mark, right up to the limit of tree growth, in the neighbourhood of 18,000. But owing to local physiography, the upper 3000 ft or so of this zone is mostly arid and conforms more closely with the steppe country of the Tibetan plateau.

And in as much as each of these altitudinal zones harbours a characteristic and more or less easily recognisable avifauna of its own, they are of the greatest importance and interest to the student of bird ecology. This study in Sikkim assumes special interest by virtue of the close parallelism that is seen to exist between the vegetation of the Eastern Himalayas and Malaya on the one hand, and that of the rain forests of Travancore – so distantly separated from it in space – on the other. Many species of birds which have their headquarters, as it were, in Malaya and the Eastern Himalayas are also found in the humid hilly areas of south-western India after a clean break in their distribution of between 1000 and 1500 miles. The country lying in between is too dry, and therefore unsuited for their existence. They are birds of sedentary habits and comparatively feeble flight, and do not migrate at any season to any appreciable extent. Thus the only explanation for the presence of the resident populations of these typically East Himalayan birds in Travancore is that at some remote period in the geological history of India there was an unbroken stretch of moist evergreen vegetation from Sikkim right across to the south-west corner of the peninsula, and that these specialised birds were then spread continuously over the whole of this area.

Owing to its climate and geographical position and the wide range of altitudinal zonation, telescoped within a comparatively restricted space, Sikkim contains the richest bird fauna within the Indian Union, and is perhaps not excelled in this respect anywhere in the world. The number of species and subspecies of birds recorded from this small area is something over 550, which is about 25 per cent of the total number on the Indian list. It contains a great many rare and beautiful forms, not met with elsewhere at all, or which have their headquarters in Sikkim where they spill over into eastern Nepal on the one hand and into Bhutan on the other.

Changes in configuration of the land, such as the wearing down of high mountain ranges which are an important rain-producing agency, brought about a gradual desiccation of the intervening country. Thus, the same species of bird now found at the two widely separated points, namely in Sikkim and in Travancore, represents in fact relict populations which have become marooned by the disappearance of suitable life conditions in the central part of peninsular India. Zoological investigations in other branches of animal life suggest that the Satpura mountain trend, which stretches across peninsular India in a south-west–north-easterly direction, is the most likely route over which the specialised rain-forest forms of plants, mammals, birds, reptiles, torrential hill-stream fishes, and others could have reached South India.

One of the most spectacular of these far-flung species among birds is the well-named Fairy Bluebird. In size it is more or less like the Common Myna. The upper parts of the male are an almost unbelievable brilliant ultramarine blue, contrasting with the rest of the plumage which is a deep velvety black.

These delightful birds move about among the lofty treetops of the tropical zone feeding on wild fruits and berries. Their rich, mellow, percussive calls *peepit, peepit,* repeated every few seconds, soon arrest the attention of the ornithologist who is familiar with one or the other end of the bird's distributional range.

There are certain well-recognised rules or principles in the geography of animals which are of more or less universal application and which carry the force almost of natural laws. One of these, known as Bergmann's Rule, postulates that in warm-blooded animals of wide distribution the populations living nearer the Equator are smaller in size than their representatives living in more northern latitudes. Bergmann's Rule is seen in practical demonstration when resident bird populations of Sikkim are compared with their counterparts in Travancore, and the Fairy Bluebird of Sikkim offers a case in point. It is quite appreciably larger, and has a longer wing, than Travancore birds.

Another good instance of similarly broken geographical distribution, coincident with heavy rainfall and damp forest, is provided by the Great Indian Hornbill. This is a large black-and-white bird nearly the size of the vulture, notable chiefly for its enormous, clumsy, horn-shaped yellow bill. It lives in lofty humid tree-forest on a diet of wild figs and other fruit. Apart from its somewhat comical get-up, this hornbill is remarkable for its extraordinary nesting habits. The eggs are laid in a natural hollow in a tree trunk, often at heights of over 100 ft from the ground. Once the female has settled herself within, the entrance to the hollow is walled up with a cement of mud and the bird's droppings, leaving only a narrow window. The female remains thus imprisoned until some days after the young hatch out. During her term of incarceration the male works like her slave, spending his time in collecting food, which is passed in to her through the narrow opening left in the wall.

One of the objects of the present expedition to Sikkim in selecting winter for its fieldwork up in the mountains was to obtain first-hand data on the behaviour, food, and feeding habits of high-altitude birds, and on the general life conditions there at a season when plant and insect life are at their lowest ebb, and when most lizards and small mammals – the normal food of birds of prey – are underground in winter sleep. Such data is practically non-existent on account of the discomforts an expedition would have to face under adverse weather conditions during winter time.

Perhaps our most interesting experience was meeting the Grandala as low down as 9000 ft above sea level, in both the Lachen and Lachung valleys of North Sikkim. The Grandala, for which unfortunately no more understandable English name exists, is a bird somewhat smaller than the Common Myna, rather of the shape and size of the Blue Rock Thrush. Its precise family position is not yet clear. Some ornithologists consider it nearest to the Thrushes, others place it with the starlings or mynas, while yet others believe that its nearest relation is the American Bluebird of the genus *Sialia*. In its flight and general behaviour it resembles all these three, and its nesting habits are akin to those of the Blue Rock Thrush. A detailed anatomical study, for which the expedition was able to collect the necessary material, will perhaps settle the point.

The male Grandala is a truly gorgeous creature, deep purple-blue and bright ultramarine. The female is brown, spotted with white, and has a white bar in the wing, which is especially noticeable in flight. The normal summer habitat of this species is between 14,000 and 20,000 ft in the Himalayas from Garhwal to south-eastern Tibet, and in the mountains of Western China. Its usual diet is said to be purely insectivorous, but when forced down in winter to the comparatively low elevations where we found the vast restless flocks, they appear to live exclusively on the sour yellow abundant berries of the shrub (*Hippophae salicifolia*) which grows gregariously on the hillsides.

Several species of game birds live in the high mountains of Sikkim, of which the pheasants are the most beautiful and attractive. The three commonest species are the Monal, the Tragopan, and the Blood Pheasant.

A distinguished professor of Zoology in Cambridge University has recently carried out a series of ingeniously devised experiments on the palatability of birds. His general finding is that brightly coloured plumage is correlated with unpalatability. This verdict will be supported independently and wholeheartedly by all who have tried to dine off the Blood Pheasant – gaudy in his livery of crimson-splashed yellowy green.

7

Bird Life of the Chilka Lake*

SITUATED IN THE state of Orissa, at about the same latitude on the eastern seaboard of India as Bombay city is on the west, is the Chilka Lake, a large sheet of shallow brackish water well known to every wildfowler, and a favourite Xmas haunt of Calcutta sportsmen.

The lake is, in fact, a brackish lagoon or backwater – of the sort that is more familiar on the coast of Travancore in South India. It is separated from the Bay of Bengal by a long sandbar, some two miles across at its widest, and hardly more than 200 yards at its narrowest point. A narrow neck or opening connects it with the sea about its middle, through which the sea flows in at high tide, producing the salinity. In the monsoon months the rivers Bhārgavi and Dayā empty their flood waters into the lagoon at its northern end, bringing down large quantities of fertile silt to form flat shallow islets that shift from year to year with the vicissitudes of the ceaseless tug of war that goes on between the rivers and the sea. The area covered by the water of the lake is some 350 sq. miles in the dry season, and increases by a further 100 sq. miles or so during the monsoon when, due to the seasonal inundation brought down by the rivers, the water becomes practically fresh.

*4 November1955, Bombay, for Cuttack.

The average depth of the lake is between 3 and 5 ft and scarcely anywhere over 6 ft. These flat silt islands are often barely above water level, and the older perennial ones are covered with reeds and grasses. The lake is set amongst some of the most picturesque scenery to be found in this part of the country, with high green hills bordering it, particularly in the west and south. On the eastern end of the lake, paddy is extensively grown on the silt formations, where it produces bountiful crops. The lake abounds in fish of many kinds and is the centre of a flourishing fishing industry which supplies the Calcutta market some 300 miles away, and other distant parts of the country. From this overall picture of the lake it will be seen that the Chilka possesses all the ingredients that go into the making of a first class wildfowl jheel: the large expanse of shallow water studded with numerous shallow silt islets under sedges and grass affords the necessary cover and food for wild ducks, geese, and snipe, while the extensive paddy cultivation at hand for raiding at night furnishes the wildfowl with easy living. The slight brackishness of the water, and the plentiful supply of fish and other small aquatic animals which the lake holds, offer added attraction to numerous other species of waterbirds as well – pelicans, storks of several species, herons, egrets, darters, cormorants, etc. All in all, therefore, whether to the sportsman with the gun or to the non-violent birdwatcher with his binoculars, the Chilka offers enviable opportunities, and it is a popular resort of sportsmen and bird lovers from near and distant parts of the country during the winter months.

Among the sporting birds most coveted by the Xmas and New Year shikari are the two species of wild geese that regularly visit the lake in large numbers at the season of festivity, when roast goose on the menu happens to be especially topical and popular. From accounts of competent sportsmen with long experience of duck shooting on the Chilka, it appears that the Grey Lag

Goose is the first to arrive. The Grey Lag, it may be mentioned, looks exceedingly like the grey form of our domestic goose, only slightly smaller. It is believed to be the original ancestor of all domesticated geese, just as the Red Junglefowl, found in the forested hills in the surroundings of the lake, is the father-and-mother of all breeds of the domestic "murghi". The Barheaded Goose, which can be easily recognised by its white head and neck and two conspicuous broad black bars across the nape, follows somewhat later, being well in just before mid-December. The numbers of the two species even up at the end of the year when the gunfire is at its heaviest, the Barhead becoming progressively commoner thereafter. To me the most astonishing thing about the Barheaded Goose has always seemed its extreme wariness while in its winter quarters in India, and the unbelievable tameness the same birds exhibit once they are across the Himalayas, back on their breeding grounds in Tibet! All birds learn within a very short time where they are safe and where not, and which human can be trusted and who must be avoided. On a visit to their nesting grounds in the environs of the lakes Manasarovar and Rakhastal in western Tibet a few years ago, I was astounded and charmed to find these same Barheaded Geese, which in India are usually difficult to approach even within reasonable rifle shot, grazing unconcernedly within fifty yards of my tent pitched on the grassy margin of a small lake. The remarkable thing is perhaps not so much their tameness in a country where they are normally unmolested by the natives, who are all Buddhists, as their sudden change of behaviour immediately upon entering their winter quarters south of the Himalayan Range where bitter experience has taught them that taking liberties with humans does not pay.

In among the hordes of these Barheads and Grey Lags that visit the Chilka some rare species of geese also turn up occasionally. The pretty little White-fronted Goose, smaller than the Grey Lag, with a white forehead and broad black crescent-shaped markings on its belly, has been obtained once, and may, for all we know, be less common as a sparse visitor than has been observed, though this is its most southerly record in India. Numerous species of migratory wild ducks already begin to arrive by the end of September. The commonest species, and the one that perhaps figures most prominently in the game bags, is the Gadwal. It is followed closely by the Shoveler, the Wigeon, the Pintail, and the Garganey or Bluewinged Teal. The Common or Green-winged Teal is comparatively scarce, the other migratory species being chiefly the three Pochards – Redcrested, Tufted, and Common. The Mallard is seen in small numbers in certain years and the Brahminy Duck or Ruddy Sheldrake is quite plentiful periodically. Once in a way the common Sheldrake turns up in considerable numbers. It is a rare winter visitor to India and the few records we have are confined mostly to Bihar and Bengal. It is possible that this duck visits the Chilka in small numbers more or less regularly since it has been recorded in different years by several observers. It is a strikingly patterned black-and-white duck with a peculiar upturned cherry-red bill. The drake has a prominent knob on the forehead, rather like the comb of the Nukta, but of the same bright colour as the bill.

Among the resident species of duck, that is to say duck that spend the entire year in this country and breed here, the ones commonly met with are the Spotbill and the Lesser Whistling Teal, the latter usually in fair numbers. The Nukta, which is the largest of our non-migratory ducks, and the Cotton Teal, which is the smallest, are rare but occasionally also seen. The Nukta is almost as large as a small goose, with a prominent knob or comb projecting upward from the base of the bill in the male, which becomes greatly swollen in the breeding season. The Cotton Teal, scarcely bigger than a pigeon, looks very much like a diminutive goose in general outline, the short bill deep at the base, and the shape of the head and neck being particularly reminiscent of that bird. Dwarf Goose-Teal, as it is sometimes called, is a more appropriate name for it than a great many bird names usually are. One of the greatest charms of the Chilka is the possibility, always present, of all sorts of unexpected birds turning up amongst the hordes of the more humdrum species.

Unfortunately, we possess practically no information about the life history of the resident waterbirds of the Chilka, except the bare fact of their occurrence in the cold season. The conditions in the environs of the lake and the abundance of the fish supply available throughout the year leave little doubt that many species of waterbirds like storks, herons, egrets, and cormorants must find congenial conditions for nesting in its vicinity. But we do not know what species actually do so, and anything about the extent of their breeding colonies. The ornithological survey of Orissa state, which I had the opportunity of carrying out a few years ago, and whose report is still under preparation, worked the Chilka area during the winter only, and was therefore unable to procure any of the desired data. The non-sporting resident waterbirds that were observed by the survey were Storks – chiefly Painted and Open-billed – Grey and Purple Herons, all the three white egrets – the Large the Smaller and the Little – Darters or Snake-birds, and cormorants of at least two species, namely, the Large Cormorant and the Small. A flock of Pelicans was also seen a long way off which could either be the resident Spotted-billed – one of whose nearest known breeding places to the Chilka is the Kollair Lake – or the Eastern Rosy Pelican which visits us in winter from regions to the north of the Himalayas. Besides these, small numbers of Spoonbills and White Ibises were also seen.

Considering the richness of the Chilka in fish, and the economic importance of the indigenous fishing industry, it seems a pity that no proper investigation has been carried out on the effect of fish-eating birds on the fisheries. For although it is obvious that birds like pelicans, herons, and cormorants must exercise considerable influence on the stock, it is not necessary that this influence should always be of a harmful nature. Careful research on the food and feeding habits of several species of fish-eating birds, in the U.S.A. and various European countries, have produced results which have utterly confounded their accusers as enemies of the fishing industry. The heron, for example, which was previously branded as one of the major culprits, has not only been completely exonerated, but by a co-ordinated analysis of its stomach contents and a study of its feeding habits has, on the contrary, been shown to be actively beneficial.

The heron's method of hunting is, as you may see on the Chilka any day, to wade into shallow water along the edge, and there to "freeze" like a statue with poised bill and neck, watching patiently to jab at a fish blundering within range. The investigators of the Fish & Wild Life Service of the U.S. Department found that due to its habit of feeding in shallow water, the major part of the heron's diet consists of cat fishes and other normally worthless species that live in the shallows close to the shore and are themselves largely predaceous on the fry of fishes of economic value which keep to deeper water, beyond the zone of the heron's hunting.

This is an example of how necessary it is to conduct a proper scientific investigation before a bird is stigmatised as harmful and proclaimed for destruction. The case of the heron is on a par with that of birds of prey. Practically ever since man turned his attention to the preservation of his animal food resources, birds of prey have been looked upon as his arch-enemies, since they also killed the birds and other animals which he wished to preserve for himself. By an impartial scientific study of the food and feeding habits of birds of prey as a class, it has now been convincingly shown that the vast majority of hawks live chiefly on rats and mice, or on sickly or disabled birds. By the large-scale destruction of these harmful and prolific rodents, they do the greatest service to agriculture, and thus deserve our careful protection rather than extermination.

8

Watching Birds*

FIFTY YEARS AGO bird watching in India was nowhere as popular, or indeed respectable, as it has become today. In my younger days I would time and again fall in with persons who left me with a feeling, as they withdrew, that they were inwardly tapping a pitying finger on their foreheads. Their first glimpse of me very often was, it is true, of a distinctly shabby khaki-clad individual of the garage mechanic type, wandering leisurely and rather aimlessly about the countryside and surreptitiously peeping into bushes, and holes in tree-trunks and earth banks. At times they would see me suddenly rooted to the ground with a pair of ponderous looking binoculars glued to my eyes for long stretches of time. I don't doubt that some of them, at least, suspected all these hole-and-corner tactics to be conducted on behalf of some foreign power with nefarious designs. However, curiosity, or maybe the thrill of confronting a dangerous criminal caught in the act, would draw them closer to me. An amiable but rather vague conversation would ensue which usually left my new acquaintance unconvinced.

Watching birds? Surely sane people don't do that! Do you kill and eat them? No? Do you sell them or export them, dead or

*10 October 1985, Delhi. This broadcast is largely excerpted from "Bird Watching" (1942), and "Bird Watching" (1952), both in this section.

alive, whole or in parts? Do you catch them and cage them, and teach them to talk or turn somersaults? Do you make medicines out of them, or how do you convert them into hard cash? "Well, if it is none of these things," I could imagine them saying to themselves, "then surely our suspicion was correct. Let's move on before he turns violent." And in this they were probably wise. I remember one occasion many years ago – it was the torrid month of April in northern India. I had been trying for the best part of a whole morning to locate the nest and young of a Blackbellied Finch-Lark in a parched, shingly riverbed. After what seemed an endless vigil, binoculars glued to my eyes, the male bird, insect in bill, who had been flitting about evasively from stone to stone in the vicinity, showed signs of getting over his nervousness. It looked as if at last he was about to visit the hidden nest. Just at this moment, an individual who had apparently been snooping on me from a distance, burst in on the scene, noisily crunching the gravel under his hob-nails, and with gushing friendliness enquired if that was a telephone I was using and who I was trying to call up! Now, ornithologists are, as a rule, mild and harmless individuals, but that unknown one, I am sure, has never failed to testify that they are prone to break out into inexplicable fits of unprovoked anger.

There is an indefinable pleasure in meeting in the flesh a bird that one has seen in a picture or read about in a book, or heard of in legend or poetry. There is greater satisfaction in running to earth the builder of a strange nest that you happen to have come across on your rambles, or in shadowing and finally discovering the producer of an unfamiliar song you have heard. The pleasure is greater when you can discover some peculiarity in the habits of a bird: what it eats and how it procures its food; its behaviour towards enemies, towards others of its kind; towards its young; how it reacts to danger or adapts itself to changed natural conditions, and so on.

All this is what makes bird watching a pursuit for the out of doors that is without rival. It can be indulged in by everybody with pleasure and profit. You don't need to be a trained zoologist to enjoy birds or to watch them and be able to contribute valuable information to ornithology. I remember when I travelled through Europe in the late 1950s how amazed I was to discover the large numbers of amateur birdwatchers in those countries. Many of these young men and women were keen and knowledgeable workers and were doing some excellent fieldwork on their local birds. There was, for instance, one unforgettable young man, a barber's assistant in Basel, who was working on a problem connected with the population dynamics of different species of titmouse, under the direction of a university professor! He would crop his customers' hair all week long and wait impatiently for the clock to strike one on Saturday afternoons. Immediately the shop was shut, he would jump on his bicycle with his binoculars and his rucksack (containing his nets, rings, weighing scales, and other paraphernalia) and make a beeline for the forest four miles away, which was the scene of his operations. He would plunge into the investigation the rest of Saturday and all Sunday and return to attack his customers' heads and beards on Monday morning!

In spite of the wealth of birdlife in the country, bird watching did not become popular among Indians until quite recently. Most of the pioneering birdwatchers in India were Britishers who had grown up in a natural-history tradition in their own country. One of our major obstacles to the popularisation of bird watching was the absence of good colour illustrated field guides. Most people were intimidated by the necessity of poring over lengthy descriptions or musty museum specimens to be able to identify a bird. With the advent of well-illustrated field guides, identification of birds became simpler, and more and more people are taking to watching and enjoying birds.

I am often asked by novices how they should begin meaningful bird watching. Here are a few tips:

Upon meeting a strange bird it is good to take down as detailed notes as possible, on the spot and while you are observing the bird. Size, colour, pattern, and comparative lengths of the different parts, colour of eyes, bill and legs – notes of that sort are most helpful. Also whether the bird was on the ground or in a tree, whether solitary or in a flock, and so on. The more detailed and accurate your notes are, the greater your chances of correct identification later. Leave nothing to memory. Memory is a thoroughly unreliable jade and delights in playing the most fantastic tricks to lead you astray.

Personally I consider it almost as important to note the environment in which a bird is seen, and also its preoccupation at the time, since these clues narrow down the range of possibilities a great deal. To take an example. A bird is described to you as black and slightly larger than a Jungle Crow, and with a pointed bill. If you are told at the same time that several such birds were sitting on a dead tree in the middle of a tank sunning themselves with wings outstretched and open, you are almost certain that it cannot be any species of crow. If you further learn that the bird flew down and alighted on the water, you are left with little doubt that the bird was a cormorant.

Unfortunately no book is able to convey to you with any degree of adequacy the song or call of a bird. Nothing short of a tape recording can give a proper idea. And considering the absence of such recordings for Indian birds, the only alternative is to familiarise yourself with calls and songs in the field and note them down in your own way so that at least you yourself will be able to recognise the caller when you hear it next time.

The royal road to learning bird identification is of course to be out in the field with someone who, even though not expert, is at least a birdwatcher familiar with the birds of that area. In identifying a bird observers must exercise scrupulous care because the positive determination of the species is essential if any notes concerning it are to be of value. Many a useful observation is ruined by faulty or doubtful identification, and once a mistake finds its way into published literature it is seldom possible to correct it effectively, or to repair its author's reputation.

However, recognising a bird in the field is not the end of bird study; it is merely a means to the end. It is just the ABC – the beginning of a fascinating hobby which enables us to learn more about the living bird and its ecology.

PART II

SEASONS FOR BIRDS

"Yet the riddle of migration has enthralled Man and held his wonderment through the ages"

– Sálim Ali, Radio Talk, "Birds: The International Wayfarers" (1941)

Ringing migratory birds.
(*Photo by Belinda Wright*)

Among waterbirds in Keoladeo National Park, Rajasthan, 1980.
(*Photo by Peter Jackson*)

1

Birds

The International Wayfarers*

MOST PEOPLE, WHEREVER they may reside in this country, and even those who are only moderately observant and little interested in matters connected with Natural History, have noticed the marked influx of birds that takes place every year chiefly between September and November. The abundance of birds during the winter, in places where there seemed to be none a couple of months before, is too striking a phenomenon to escape anybody. The species eagerly sought after by the shikari – the snipe, duck, geese, cranes, quails, and many other game birds – together with the hosts of lesser fry that interest him little or not at all – like the sandpipers, tree-warblers, larks, pipits, wagtails, and numerous other species – all seem to pop up suddenly from nowhere almost overnight.

The man in the street just takes the birds for granted: they come at this season because it is the will of Allah that they should. Whence they come is none of his business, while why or how they do it is clearly the birds' own affair. Yet the riddle of migration has enthralled Man and held his wonderment through the ages. A hard-headed scientific outlook is now helping to dispel

*28 December 1941. Broadcast from Lahore.

many of the fanciful notions held by our forebears, but it is clear that some of the vital mysteries involved will continue to remain in the realm of speculation. A belief very generally held in the past, evoked by the seasonal appearance and disappearance of birds, was that small species like the swallow and the cuckoo buried themselves in mud at the bottom of ponds to sleep out the winter, whence they emerged with the first signs of favourable weather in spring.

By bird migration is implied the periodic exodus of birds from a given area to avoid the rigours of climate, and their return to the same area at another season when conditions as regards weather and food supply again become favourable. It is an axiom in Nature that migratory birds always nest in the colder portion of their geographical range. Thus those birds that visit India during the cold weather return to the lands beyond the Himalayas – to Central Asia and Siberia – when our summer begins. The colder portion of their range really is their home. In the southern hemisphere the order is reversed and the migrants move northward – towards the equator – to escape the inhospitable conditions of the southern winter. But it must not be supposed that migration involved long journeys only. The movements may vary from no more than a few miles (such as from a couple of thousand feet in the Himalayan foothills down into the North Indian Plains and back again), to several thousand miles either way, as is the case with many of our wild ducks and geese. The longest migratory journey known is performed twice every year by the Arctic Tern, a sea bird, which travels right across the world from the Arctic winter to the Antarctic summer and back again – a distance of over 11,000 miles each way.

The advantages gained by a bird resident in northern climes by migrating to warmer countries on the approach of winter are fairly self-evident. The move enables it to avoid the cold and stormy weather of the northern latitudes, the shortening daylight hours available for procuring food, and from the conditions that bring about a scarcity of its food supply such as the freezing of water and snow enshrouding the ground. The return to northern lands (or southern in the case of the southern hemisphere) in spring, following the luxuriant sprouting of vegetation, provides it with an abundance of food and all the conditions necessary for the successful rearing of a family including uncongested nesting sites and long hours of daylight in which to forage for its voracious young.

Two of the many migration puzzles which continue to baffle investigators are, firstly, in the absence of Messrs Thos Cook or other international travel agencies, what tells a bird where to go and spend the winter months? Secondly, how does a bird find its way to this destination? In many cases, young birds of the first season without any previous experience either of the route or of the goal, often thousands of miles away, accomplish the journey without undue casualty through accident or misadventure, and with remarkable accuracy.

An astounding feature is the precision and regularity with which birds return to their breeding locality – their home – after far-flung and often intercontinental wanderings, year after year. It has been found that swallows whose home is in Europe and which spend the northern winter in South Africa, often return not only to the same province or county, but even to the identical farmstead or building for nesting purposes every summer, covering distances of 6000 miles or more each way during the interval. This is the case with many other true migrants as well. Prolonged observations in many parts of India on the appearance and disappearance of migrant birds point to the astonishing regularity and punctuality, almost to the day, with which particular species arrive in particular localities. This seems the more amazing when we take into account the enormous distances covered by many of them and involving as it does the hazardous crossing over the lofty Himalayan barrier.

The method of marking or "ringing" birds as an aid to the study of their geographical movements has, in recent years, been very widely and profitably pursued in Europe and America. Bird-ringing – or "banding" as it is called in the land of the Almighty Dollar – consists of fastening a light aluminium ring of appropriate size stamped with the ringer's address and a serial number to the leg of a trapped or netted bird, or of a young bird before it leaves the nest. A detailed record is kept of this individual in a special register showing the species, male or female, adult or young, locality and date of ringing, and so on. The bird is then released. It happens that a small percentage of these ringed birds – varying from one to fifteen and sometimes more, according to species and distance flown – are subsequently killed or captured in near and distant lands and their rings returned, or the inscriptions on them communicated, to the marking station with information as to the exact locality where recovered, date, and other particulars. When a sufficiently large number of such recovery records has been obtained it is possible gradually to build up positive knowledge of the routes followed on migration by different species, the time taken on the journeys, the length of the stages and total distances flown, the longevity of individual birds, and a great many important facts that would be impossible to learn authentically in any other way. Thus, ringing has enabled us to say that the Black-headed Gull (common on our western seaboard in winter) may live for at least twenty-six years. So feeble and unimpressive a flier as the Coot is shown to have covered a distance of 164 miles in a single day. A Coot ringed in Indore state was killed in Russia after it had accomplished a journey of at least 1500 miles, presumably in stages, and crossed over the Himalayas. Of great interest to local listeners will be the record of the recovery near Lahore, a few years ago, of a Rose-coloured Starling or Tilyer which had been ringed as a nestling in Eastern Hungary (3000 miles away) only a few months previously.

The ringing of White Storks in Western Germany and East Prussia has established conclusively that the E. Prussian birds migrate to Africa by a south-eastern route through the Balkans, while the West German storks travel by a south-western route through Spain, the two "armies" making a pincer movement round the Sahara. It was the recovery of a German-ringed stork in Bikaner a few years ago (3600 miles from the place of ringing) which provided the first definite proof that some at least of the White Storks that visit us in winter are "Made in Germany". Comparatively little ringing work has so far been done in India, but the results obtained from it as well as from recoveries here of Russian and German ringed birds, are of very great interest since they furnish the only positive confirmation of the hitherto conjectured origin of some of our winter visitors. We now know that many species of our migrant ducks breed in Siberia at distances of 2000 to 3000 miles and more from their winter quarters in India. A Glossy Ibis ringed at Astrakhan, on the northern shores of the Caspian Sea, was killed near Nasik (at least 2500 miles distant), while a Green Sandpiper (a bird of about the size of a Quail) had flown from Kazan near Moscow to Kottayam in Travancore, 3600 miles in a straight line on the map.

The Bombay Natural History Society would welcome co-operation from listeners in their Wildfowl Ringing Scheme. Any of you who are interested and in a position to help in this important and useful enquiry will be gladly supplied with rings, blank schedules, and instructions on application to the Honorary Secretary. The Russians have, within recent years in their territory, ringed ducks of many kinds on a large scale. Should any sportsman obtain a bird bearing a ring with grotesque-looking outlandish characters, he is requested to be good enough to forward it to the Bombay Natural History Society. Many thousands of Rose-coloured Starlings (Tilyer) have also been marked on their breeding grounds in Central Asia and Eastern Hungary, and it is more than probable that some of them may be recovered in India.

Fantastic notions have been entertained in the past regarding the speed and height at which migratory birds fly. Estimates of 150 to 250 miles per hour in the case of many small birds were not unusual, and it was moreover believed that it was of some particular advantage to birds to fly at stupendous heights above the earth – for locating landmarks, minimising air resistance, and in other ways. Modern devices such as the aeroplane, speed indicators, altimeters, and other instruments used in anti-aircraft gunnery have shown how greatly exaggerated those estimates were. Velocities naturally vary with species of bird and prevailing meteorological conditions. The average cruising speed of wild ducks and geese, which appear to move at terrific speed, has been found to be actually between 40 and 50 miles per hour as against the old estimate of well over 100. Under favourable conditions their speed may reach 50 to 60 m.p.h. In the case of the smaller birds the old estimates have proved to be even more inaccurate.

It is also clear that actually, except when lofty mountain ranges have to be crossed, migrating birds prefer to fly under 1300 feet and very rarely over 3000 ft above ground. Some species indeed habitually fly much lower when no trees or similar obstacles have to be avoided, often almost skimming the surface of the water on sea crossings in calm weather.

Non-stop flights of 2000 to 3000 miles are regularly made by the Golden Plover and the Japanese Snipe. The former, which visits India also during the cold weather, breeds in Western Alaska and N-E. Siberia and is a regular visitor to the Hawaiian Islands. There is no land in between these regions on which it could rest.

Similarly the Japanese Snipe spends the northern winter in E. Australia and Tasmania, flying over the ocean in a single "hop", and back home to breed.

One such long-distance flyer among our Indian birds is the Woodcock – an overgrown snipe much prized by sportsmen – which breeds in the Himalayas and spends the winter in the Nilgiri and other hills of South India. Since the species has only very rarely been found anywhere in between, it is clear that the shortest distance it must cover in a single hop is not less than 1500 miles.

It has often been suggested and long believed that, on their biannual journeys to and from the plains of India, migrating birds use the valleys of the larger rivers as highways in order to avoid the hazards of flying over the Himalayas. Evidence obtained by Tibetan explorers and Himalayan mountaineers proves this belief to be without foundation. Their observations suggest that the birds fly indiscriminately over and across some of the highest parts of the Himalayas without much inconvenience and are able thereby to shorten their journeys very considerably.

When one considers the immense scale on which bird migration takes place in India, the meagreness of our knowledge in every branch of it seems deplorable. A co-ordinated effort by observers and students of birds in different parts of the country and bird-ringing on a large scale are the only ways in which the various problems can be tackled satisfactorily.

The migrations of birds are really an international affair, and real progress is only possible by a close co-operation between the various countries affected. The wanderings range over large tracts of the globe, therefore the only adequate study of their movements can be the one which takes in their entire geographical range regardless of political boundaries. Much useful international co-operation had been achieved in this investigation during record years until this war suddenly brought about total eclipse!

2

Birds in August*

SINCE I SPOKE to you last month it has rained cats and dogs. Village tanks everywhere have turned into little inland seas. In many places the low-lying country is under water. Only the bunds separating the fields and the tops of tiny mounds stick out here and there looking like parts of a miniature archipelago. In one place I even noticed a boat taking people across to and from their house in the midst of fields now under knee-deep water. All this abundance of water is naturally what the frogs and fishes have been praying for throughout the dry season while they lay buried many feet below the dry and thirsty soil. They came up immediately the rain softened the ground and water collected into pools and puddles, and their first care was to lay their eggs. Tadpoles, young frogs, and old frogs and fish of every age and size are now teeming everywhere and are having the time of their lives, but in the midst of life they are in death: for there is, every now and again, unceasing through day and night alike, a little splash and commotion in the water – the sudden jab of a dagger-pointed bill – and one of their number vanishes. For while the frogs and fishes were praying for rain, the waterbirds have been praying for the frogs and fishes: now both prayers have been answered.

*28 July 1942, Bombay. The opening phrase "since I spoke to you last month" probably refers to the talk titled "Birds in July" dated 30 June 1942, listed in the author's files but now lost. See Introduction.

The several kinds of egrets and paddy birds known indiscriminately as "Bagla", the cormorants (*pan-kowla*), the jacanas, moorhens, and dabchicks all depend for their food on water animals, be they frog, fish, snail, insect, or worm. The jacanas – of which we have two different kinds common on most tanks – the Pheasant-tailed and the Bronze-winged, are truly remarkable creatures. Their enormous feet remind you rather of Charlie Chaplin's famous shoes. However, comical as they seem, the object of these outsize toes is not merely to amuse you. They serve a far more useful purpose. They help to spread out the weight of the bird so that it does not sink below the surface of the water when trotting along over floating lotus leaves and other vegetation in search of its food.

All these waterbirds are now leading a merry life of ease and plenty. Food is abundant and easy to procure. The conditions are just right for them to build their nests and bring up their families. The various kinds of egrets, herons, cormorants, and other waterbirds usually select some large leafy tree, such as a tamarind, and nest in mixed company. On a single tree, which for some reason or other is often situated in or near a village, you may sometimes count fifty nests or more. They belong to four or five different kinds of birds, all of whom seem to live as neighbours on perfectly friendly terms. When the young birds born in this colony – or heronry, as it is called – are old enough to leave the nest and clamber about amongst the branches, but before they are able to fly away, there is usually great noise and confusion on the tree. The families get so mixed up that it must be impossible for parents and offspring to recognise each other. At this stage it happens, therefore, that the old birds arriving with food simply shove it down the throats of the first hungry youngsters that beg for it, and are off again to fetch more, trusting to luck for the welfare of their own young.

There are two or three large tamarind trees quite close to Borivli Railway Station, on the eastern side, which are now covered with several species of egrets and their nests, and provide good opportunities for watching. The tamarind tree just outside Bandra Railway Station is also occupied in most years, and there are several trees growing in Thana town which are the usual nesting haunts of waterbirds.

The tall coarse grass and paddy plants, already about waist-high, supply building material to the Common Weaver Bird or Baya for his wonderful retort-shaped woven nests which hang in clusters from date and palmyra palms, and from babool trees, all over the countryside. I am sure you all know who the Baya is, or at least are familiar with his cleverly built nests. During half the year the cock and hen Baya are alike to look at – very like the female House Sparrow. But when the nesting season comes round and the male has put on his wedding suit of golden yellow and dark brown, he becomes a splendid looking handsome fellow. If you meet him between June and November you will hardly recognise him, so greatly does he differ from his soberly dressed wife. Soon after the rains set in, the nesting activities of the Baya commence. The gaily attired cock birds constantly fly out in a party from the selected nest tree, tear off strips from the edge of the paddy leaf with their bills, and fly back with the material, all together, in a sort of egg-and-spoon race. It is an object lesson to watch the little weaver at work. The architecture or plan on which the nest is built, and the intelligent manner in which the strips are woven in with the help of bill and feet, are astonishing. The rough saw-edges of the grass would cut your skin if you rubbed your finger over them. It is this roughness that prevents the weaving of the nest from slipping loose once the material has been tightly pulled into position. And this also is what makes the fabric so compact and strong. No water can get through it, and no amount of swinging in the strong monsoon winds can do it any harm. If you try pulling to pieces an old Baya nest you will realise how strongly woven it is.

Inside every Baya nest is always to be found a small quantity of mud stuck to the side. The purpose of this is unknown. Your mali will of course tell you that it is for the Baya to stick fireflies in, to light up its nest at night. But this is just your mali's tale; don't you believe it!

Watching a colony of Bayas at work in the earlier stages – when the nests have just begun – you will soon be struck by the fact that all the workers are cocks in their brilliant wedding suits, and that there are no hens present to help them. But the birds seem to enjoy their labour thoroughly. There is a great deal of merry noise and chatter going on, and every now and again all the builders flutter their wings and join in a community chorus which ends in a long drawn *chee-ee-ee*. When the nests are about half-built they are, so to say, ready "To be Let". A party of hen birds, anxious to lay eggs and bring up a family, see the advertisement, as it were, and arrive on the scene. They hop from nest to nest and inspect them carefully. If one of the ladies takes a fancy to a particular nest she just decides to stay. This is her way of telling the builder that she has consented to marry him. From now on you will see her helping her partner in his task, and the couple complete their home together. She spends her time mostly on the interior, preparing the chamber where the eggs and the family will come. When the nest is ready she lays two or three white eggs in it, and sits on them herself. The husband's part is done and he finds himself out of a job. But he does not like this life of idleness, and soon commences to build himself a second nest nearby. In a few days' time another female also on the look-out for a desirable home comes along to inspect. If she is satisfied with the half-built nest she "moves in" and becomes Wife No. 2. Sometimes one cock gets himself three or four wives in this way.

The Tailor-bird is another clever builder. He is the Dirzee of whom many of you have doubtless read in Kipling's *Jungle Book*. The Tailor has also been waiting for the monsoon in order to begin his work. But unlike the Baya he has not been waiting for his building material but actually for suitable places to build in. The rains bring up a variety of large-leaved weeds and creepers everywhere, and it is now also that the enormous leaves of the teak tree come out. These large leaves are what the Tailor requires for his home. He draws the edges of a leaf together, sometimes even using two leaves or more – and cleverly sews them up to form a kind of funnel or cone – something like what you buy your anna's worth of roasted monkeynuts in. The little craftsman collects silk cotton from the pods of the Simal tree and twists them into strands which serve as thread for the purpose of the stitching. His slender bill does the work of a needle. The Tailor-bird's nest is a work of art. The thread, after being passed through the edges of the leaf and drawing them tightly together, is knotted at both ends so as to keep the sewing in position. Within the safety of this leaf-cone a tiny cup-shaped nest is made of soft fibres and cotton wool in which three little eggs are laid. The whole thing is usually so beautifully hidden among the surrounding leaves that it is difficult to spot the nest unless you have watched the bird's comings and goings.

In size the Tailor-bird is smaller than the sparrow. It is greenish-brown above, white below, with a reddish-brown cap on its head. Its distinctive feature is the long narrow tail which is carried at a jaunty angle, partly cocked. Cock and hen look alike; they go about in pairs hopping from branch to branch in shrubbery in search of tiny insects. The loud calls *towhit, towhit, towhit* or *pretty, pretty, pretty* constantly uttered are some of the most familiar bird voices of the countryside. Nearly every garden in Bombay city and suburbs, and in the plains generally, has a pair or two of Tailor-birds in residence. They are trusting and fearless little creatures and will often nest in a potted croton plant in the verandah, or in a mango seedling growing under the wall of a bungalow with the inmates brushing past it many times a day.

The Tailor-bird has two near cousins, commonly seen in the open scrub jungle of the suburbs. They are of about the same size and bear an unmistakable family resemblance to the Dirzee. One of these is the Ashy Wren-Warbler, bluish-slaty above, pale brownish-white below. The other is the Indian Wren-Warbler which is an insignificant pale brown and dirty white. They have a peculiar up-and-down laboured flight and they always give you the impression that the long tail is too heavy a load to carry. They both build "tailored" nests rather similar to the Dirzee's in low bushes, and are now active with their domestic duties.

Over the flooded paddy fields and about the newly formed marshes a large and handsome bird of prey is now frequently to be seen sailing on motionless wings, and pouncing now and again on some unsuspecting frog or land crab. This is the Brahminy Kite, a bird of the same size as the Pariah Kite, but with a rounded instead of forked tail which is so characteristic of the Pariah. When full grown, its head, neck, and breast are pure white while the wings are bright brick-red or chestnut. Young birds are brown and look very like the Pariah Kite, but you can always tell them when they are flying by the rounded shape of their tail. During the dry months the Brahminy prefers to dwell in the neighbourhood of the harbour and docks where it gets a comfortable living by snatching scraps of floating refuse thrown overboard from ships. The bird is never met far from water and as there is such an abundance of it everywhere now, thanks to the monsoon, the Brahminy has been tempted to shift inland to try a change in its menu. For besides land crabs and frogs it occasionally manages to carry off a chicken from the village and that provides an additional delicacy.

3

Birds in September*

A FAMILIAR SIGHT AT this season on the low-lying water-logged grassland that you must now splash or squelch through on any cross-country ramble is the feeding parties of Common Mynas busily hunting grasshoppers amongst the grass. These parties usually consist of five or six birds: father, mother, and three or four young. The young can be told from their elders by their slenderer build and much paler colouring. Three or four is the normal size of a Myna family. The parents sometimes bring up two breeds, one after the other, so that one pair may be responsible for an addition of six to eight in the Myna population each year. But of course all these youngsters do not live to become grown-up Mynas. Many are born weaklings and die at an early age. Others fall a prey to accidents, or to enemies such as birds of prey and cats of different kinds while they are as yet too young and silly to take care of themselves. Several of these family parties often join forces and hunt in company, making up what looks like a large flock. Every bird flock is in reality a joining-up of family parties or other smaller units that have agreed to live together for a part of the year in order to derive some common benefit. This benefit may be either protection from enemies since Union is Strength, or it may be in order to make food-getting

*18 August 1942, Bombay.

easier. In many flocks you even find that the birds are not all alike but belong to several different species, all of whom derive advantage from the joint efforts of the lot.

It is fun watching these family parties of Mynas at work on a wet grass field. They hop along swiftly and jauntily after the grasshoppers, and often jump up and chase the insects in the air for a short distance. There is no escape for the enemy: if it succeeds in dodging one bird it is sure to be snatched up by the next. In places the grass is high enough to hide the birds, so from time to time while the chase is on you see one of them spring up into the air a couple of feet to take a good look at its surroundings for any unseen danger that may be approaching. If you have observed the behaviour of a dog trying to put up some animal that it can worry in a field of corn or tall grass, you will understand what I mean.

Not so plentiful as the common Myna, but frequently met with either along with it or separately, is its first cousin the Jungle Myna. Unless you know what to look for, and look for it carefully, you may easily mix up the two. But the Jungle Myna can always be distinguished by not having the bare yellow skin round the eyes which is the "trade mark" of the common Myna, and by the presence of a peculiar upstanding black tuft of feathers on the forehead. If you are fairly near you will notice in addition that the colour of its eyes is grey.

The last month or two of the monsoon is the time when the nests of the lovely little sunbirds or Honeysuckers may be looked for. Sunbirds nest in other months of the year also, but they avoid the heaviest rain. The two common species to be found in and around Bombay, and over the greater part of the plains of India, are the Purple Sunbird and the Purple-rumped Sunbird. Both are considerably smaller than the House Sparrow in size, and are indeed amongst the smallest birds we have in India. In many of their ways they resemble the Humming-Birds of South and Central America, and I have heard people refer to them (wrongly) as Humming Birds. In reality they are not related to the Humming Birds at all. Their beautiful, glistening colours and their dainty, restless, joyful habits make them welcome and attractive visitors to every garden. They flit about from flower to flower like gems in the sunshine. They cling to the blossoms upside down and in all manner of acrobatic positions. Sometimes they also hover in front of a flower, poised stationary in the air on rapidly beating wings, while they extract the nectar and tiny insects from the corolla. The food of the Sunbirds consists principally of the sweet sugary juice, or nectar, of flowers. To extract this liquid from the flowers they are equipped with a slender, long, slightly curved bill which can probe into the narrowest flower-tubes. This specially adapted bill is further assisted in its work by the thin tube-like tongue of the Sunbird which is capable of being shot out beyond the bill-tip, rather like a snake's tongue. By means of this combination of specialised bill and tongue the Sunbird is able to suck nectar from flowers with very long and deep tubes. Like bees and other pollen- and nectar-eating insects, Sunbirds do important service to plants by fertilising their flowers. In trying to reach the nectar, the birds' throat and forehead feathers become coated with the golden pollen dust. They carry this to the next flower they visit, where it gets brushed off on to the female part of that flower, which thereafter develops into fruit and into the seeds from which other plants will grow. And thus the birds help to continue generation after generation of the plant. Unfortunately the plants that Sunbirds help to increase in this way are not always beneficial to Man's interests. For example, all of you are probably familiar with the *bandha* tree-parasite that grows so abundantly and in such large clusters on mango trees everywhere. Now, this *bandha* is not an honest plant, but it is somewhat of a low-down sneak. It fixes itself firmly on other plants and robs them of the nourishment they have laboured to obtain so that the host gradually becomes weaker and weaker while the *bandha* flourishes on its life-blood and grows exceedingly. Finally, the host-tree is able to bear it no longer and it dries up and dies. The greedy *bandha*, having killed the goose that laid the golden egg as it were, is now unable to obtain further sustenance, and so it also perishes. This plant-parasite does enormous damage to mango trees. It weakens the tree and reduces its fruit-bearing capacity. The loss it causes to mango growers must run to thousands of rupees annually. It also attacks teak trees in forest plantations and retards their growth and consequent yield of timber. But it would be a mistake to imagine that the way to get rid of the *bandha* is to kill off all Sunbirds so that no further *bandha* seeds are produced! For you must remember that, besides the nectar of flowers, Sunbirds eat a great many tiny insects as well. Some of these insects do great damage to plants and crops, and it is just possible that by destroying the insects the birds do a greater service to Man than the harm they cause indirectly by propagating the tree-parasite. The lives of all animals and plants are so intimately mixed up in a number of ways that it is foolish to take a step like killing off a certain animal in the hope of producing a direct effect upon another or others. For instance, if you see an owl or a kite carry off a chicken from your yard, it would be a foolish blunder to destroy every owl and kite that you meet just because of that. Such a course is bound to result in more harm than good. Owls and kites kill large numbers of rats, lizards, and other vermin. If you finished off all the owls and kites in your neighbourhood the rats and lizards would probably increase to such an extent that they would make your poultry-keeping impossible. Thus, to save the loss of an occasional chicken you would indirectly be destroying all your poultry!

It is therefore quite essential before any such serious step is taken with regard to killing off any species of bird or animal, or even introducing a new species from outside, to investigate with the greatest care into the food and habits of the animal you propose to tamper with. All animals fulfil some special purpose in Nature. Nature keeps her balance and never permits one animal to increase disproportionately at the cost of another. If meddlesome Man interferes with this "Balance of Nature", as it is called, he always does so at the risk of serious consequences to himself.

The Sunbird's nest is a cleverly built structure and worthy of being put in the same class as that of the Tailor Bird and its two cousins I told you of last month – the Indian and Ashy Wren-warblers. It is a little oblong or pear-shaped pouch made of fine fibres, hung from the tip of a branch in a bush or small tree. A great deal of cobwebs are used in strengthening the fabric of the nest. On the outside of the nest are stuck spiders' egg cases, caterpillar droppings, bits of papery bark, and other rubbish which make the nest look exactly like some untidy bunch of rubbish blown up by the wind. The entrance hole is on one side of the pouch, and over this a small porch or shade is usually built which must help to some extent in keeping off the rain. Most of the building work and the brooding is done by the female, but the male always keeps in the vicinity and accompanies her back and forth, constantly cheering her up by snatches of a merry little song.

Two other birds commonly nesting now are the Yellow-eyed Babbler and the spotted Munia. The former is about the size of the bulbul, perhaps slightly smaller, chestnut brown above, pure white below. It seldom enters towns, but lives in scrub country on the outskirts. Although a near relation of our familiar and untidy friend the *Satbhai*, it is altogether a superior-looking creature. If you are near enough you may see the bright yellow eye that gives it its name. It builds a compact, open, cup-shaped nest in bushes, of roots and grass, plastered neatly on the outside with cobwebs. The cup is deep, so that unless you look in directly from above you may easily miss seeing the eggs. When sitting on them the bird presses itself down into the nest so cunningly that, if approached, you hardly see it. It is only when you get quite close that you notice the end of its beak and a watchful little eye peering out at one end and its longish narrow tail sticking out at the other. The cobweb plastering keeps the nest compact and tidy and helps it to withstand the constant soaking in the rain.

The Spotted Munia is a cousin of the House Sparrow. It is only half the size of the House Sparrow but twice as respectable in appearance and habits. It is chestnut brown above, white below. The white is covered with a dense collection of hollow black rings – not spots. The bill is bluish-slate in colour, short and thick for crushing hard-shelled grain and seeds – like the sparrow's but much heavier. The Munia's nest is a ball of grass about eight inches across, with a small round entrance hole on one side. The nest is normally placed in a low thorn bush where you cannot get at it without being pricked and scratched all over. In Salsette, strangely enough, a very favourite situation is on a leaf of the palmyra or *tad* palm, sometimes as high up as forty or fifty feet. It is amusing to watch the Munias collecting building material. They tear off a strip of some coarse saw-edged grass, five or six inches long, and fly off with it trailing behind in the breeze. In a high wind the material often acts like a sail, catches the wind and drags the little carrier yards out of its course. It requires much labour and persistence on the part of the bird to bring it to the lofty nest site. The Munia lays five or six white eggs, sometimes as many as eight, which seems an extraordinarily large number for so tiny a bird. Long after the young have grown up and are able to fly about and look after themselves, the family continue to live together and return every night to roost in the old home. This I must tell you is an exception to the general rule. Birds normally occupy their nests only for a very short period of the year. It is built solely for laying eggs in and for bringing up the family, and it is abandoned as soon as it has served its purpose. Rain, wind, or cold does not stop them from sleeping out in the open, and the popular notion that they go back every night to sleep in their nests is quite wrong.

Now we are getting into the season when you must keep your eyes and ears open for incoming winter visitors. Arrivals have already commenced, early as it is. I noticed a Whimbrel and a couple of Sandpipers the other day, about a fortnight ago; more have made their appearance since, and many more are doubtless on the way. The majority of migrants, however, will not be amongst us before October. But the Wagtails and Pipits should be on our lawns and maidans before long, and you must look out for them. Mark the dates of their arrival and departure year after year and you will be astonished to find how regular and punctual they are with their time-table.

4

Birds in October*

THE END OF THE monsoon is at hand. In the northern provinces there is already a delicious tang in the air as you wake up in the morning which says that winter is just round the corner. We unfortunates in Bombay, however, have still to live through October which is usually our stickiest and most unpleasant month.

But although it may be yet awhile before our so-called cold weather makes itself felt in our bones, signs of its coming are not wanting. These signs will not be found in the thermometer hanging on your wall, but they are all the same clear and unmistakable to anyone who keeps his eyes and ears open while going his daily round. He will notice the signs though his movements may not carry him beyond the limits of his own postal district. The clearest promise of all that winter is near is given by the incoming birds. The least observant amongst you, if he has been along the seashore within the last week or so, cannot have failed to notice that on the sand at the edge of the tide, on the mudflats and among the rocks are running about little brown-and-white birds with bare slender legs – the sandpipers and sandplovers – which were not there a fortnight ago. They keep singly or in flocks, and

*29 September 1942, Bombay.

the flocks are composed of a number of different kinds of wading birds – some large, some small, some middling. They look so completely at home as they scuttle about and feed – probing their bills on the soft mud – that you would think they were born and bred here, and owned the place.

At the end of my last talk, you will remember, I asked you to keep a look-out for wagtails and pipits on our lawns and maidans. I hope you did so, and I am sure you were rewarded. Small numbers of them are now amongst us. I saw my first tree-warbler of the season as early as 24 August, and my first wagtail on 11 September. It was like meeting long-lost friends, and right glad I was to welcome them. Since then their numbers have increased somewhat, slowly but surely. Their arrivals in force, however, will not be till about the middle or end of October.

Now you may well ask: Where have all these birds been? Why have they kept away from us all these months? What makes them suddenly pop up amongst us now? How did they find their way here? These are the same questions that Man has asked himself and puzzled over for thousands of years, and they still remain unanswered, in part at any rate. For enquiring men throughout the ages have devoted long years of painstaking study to the problem of the migration of birds. In the last forty years or so the investigation has taken on a more scientific aspect. By careful observation of the movements of birds from season to season, and from one part of the world to another, and with the aid of various methods and instruments, they have succeeded in getting part of the answers, but not the whole answer.

The bare fact that many birds arrive and depart with the seasons with astonishing regularity was well known to our ancestors thousands of years ago. The ancients knew, for example, that in Europe the swallow was a common and familiar bird during summer when it nested in barns and houses. Its arrival was welcomed as the first sign of approaching summer and it was – as it still is – looked upon as a happy omen by the inmates if a swallow nested in their house. But where the swallow disappeared to when winter came round was a mystery to them. And until not so long ago there were many people who seriously believed that swallows buried themselves in the mud at the bottom of ponds, like frogs and fishes, and came out immediately the weather became warmer!

Migration is the periodical going away of birds from a part of the world where living conditions have become difficult owing to natural causes (such as the weather), to another part where conditions are more suitable. Thus, in the northern hemisphere there is a movement southwards, towards the equator, to escape the severity of winter. The birds return north when the weather gets warmer; when the snow and ice have melted from the ground, and when green grass springs up again and insect life becomes plentiful. In the southern hemisphere the movement takes the opposite direction – north, towards the warmer lands in autumn, and south when conditions again become favourable in spring.

In the case of migrant birds you must remember that the colder part of their range is always their home. The birds that spend the winter months with us in India never build nests or lay their eggs here. They always go back to their homes in the northern countries to do so when the weather there gets warmer. We see, therefore, that the chief advantage a bird derives from the habit of migrating is that it is able to live in a warm climate throughout the year; in places where there is no overcrowding and where food is plentiful, enough to go round, and easy to procure.

But one of the many things it is so difficult to understand is why birds undertake these long and perilous journey even before they are actually compelled to do so. For example, why some of the birds that have already arrived in India to spend the winter left their homes while as yet conditions there were quite bearable, and months before the severe winter set in? We cannot admit that the birds had enough sense to know in advance, that after two months or so life would become difficult, and that they therefore made up their minds to act in good time and go while the going was good. We cannot explain this, just as we cannot explain how a bird knows what kind of a nest to build when the time comes. You can hatch a Weaver Bird's (Baya's) egg in an incubator so that the young Baya has no knowledge whatsoever of what its parents looked like or in what sort of a nest its egg was laid. Yet, when the bird grows up and nesting time comes round, it will build the same complicated type of woven hanging nest that its parents built, without training or experience!

It has been observed, and is now common knowledge, that if migrant birds are kept in an aviary they grow restless and agitated when the season comes round for their wild relations to begin their migratory journeys. They fly about the cage, up and down, as if impelled by some hidden driving force. And it is not until some weeks later, when the normal time for migration is long past, that the birds again settle down to normal captive life. This happens in autumn, and again in spring, year after year, even though they may have been in captivity for a long time. There seems to be some inward urge that makes itself felt at the appropriate season.

You must not think that migration consists only of long journeys. In some cases it may mean a movement of not more than a few miles, but in other cases many hundreds or thousands of miles are travelled. Some of our tiniest migrants, the Willow-Warblers, about half the size of the House-Sparrow, often cover more than 2000 miles to reach their winter quarters in India, and perform the same return journey again, back to their homes, when our hot weather commences. The astonishing thing is that in many cases the birds undertaking this long and hazardous journey are young birds, born only a few months previously. They have no experience and no knowledge of where they are going and of how to find their way there. Sometimes they may get the guidance of their elders who have done the journey before, but the young birds often travel by themselves, strangely enough, and yet manage to reach their destination without undue casualties on the way. This is all the more mystifying when it is remembered that for long stretches of the journey the birds may have to fly over the open sea where there are no landmarks to guide even the experienced ones, and where they are at the mercy of the wind, and without any place to rest if they are tired.

Another extraordinary thing about migration is the accuracy with which birds return year after year to the same locality. Swallows, for example, after flying 6000 or 7000 miles over pathless land and sea from South Africa, find their way back to England in summer, and not only to the same county and district, but sometimes even to the same farmhouse where they had nested the year before or where they were born. In the past it was believed that migrating birds flew not only at very great heights in the air but also at terrific speeds. Modern instruments, such as are used in aeroplanes, have now enabled us to get more correct estimates. It is proved that as a rule birds do not fly above 3000 ft, and normally much lower. When flying over the sea where there are no trees, hills, and other obstacles to avoid, they often fly only a few feet above the surface. Wild ducks, which are fast and strong fliers, were formerly estimated to do over 150 miles an hour. We now find that ordinarily they do not fly at more than 40 or 50 miles per hour. And, in the case of some of the smaller birds, the old estimates were still more incorrect. The entire migratory journey is not usually performed at one stretch, but in stages of from 100 to 500 miles, depending upon size of bird and weather conditions. The birds feed and rest for a few hours at each stage before continuing. It happens sometimes, however, that in the ocean there is no land on which to alight in which case they have to fly non-stop for enormous distances. Instances are known where as much as 2000 and 3000 miles are covered in a single "hop", taking the bird forty-eight hours or more. Naturally, deaths due to exhaustion must be common on these journeys, and only the fittest and strongest birds manage to reach the end.

Now, you will naturally want to know how we can tell that an individual bird seen in India in March, for example, is the same as one you may find with nest and eggs, say in Central Siberia in July. Until the system of marking or "ringing" birds was perfected and employed on a large scale some forty years ago, this was difficult, and chiefly a matter of guesswork. The ringing system is something like the system of numbering motor cars. If in the midst of Bhuleshwar, in Bombay City, you suddenly discover a car No. DLH 4050, for example, you know at once that the car has come from Delhi. Now if you take the trouble to write to the police in Delhi you can get all the particulars about this car No. 4050; who it belongs to, what make, what horsepower, how old it is, when it was registered, and so on. This is exactly the sort of information we get from marking or ringing birds. The birds are either caught in nets if grown up, or taken in their nests before they fly. A light aluminium ring is fixed on one leg, and the bird is again set free. On this ring is stamped a number and the address of the person or society who fixes the ring. All particulars concerning this bird such as its age, sex, date, and place of ringing, and so on are entered in a special register. Now if this bird is ever caught again later on, or if it is killed or found dead by anyone in any part of the world, that fact and particulars are reported to the address on the ring. Tens of thousands of birds are now ringed every year (or were, before the war) in all parts of the world by scientific societies who keep each other informed of their activities. When a large number of ringed birds are recovered near and far, and detailed records of this sort obtained, it is possible to build up correct knowledge about the movements of the different species. They tell us of the routes followed by the birds, the time taken on the journey, the age to which individuals live, and a great many other particulars impossible to learn in any other way.

By the ringing method we have been able to learn that the wild ducks that visit the tanks and jheels of India during the cold weather go to distances of 2000 and 3000 miles in Central Asia and Siberia in summer, over and across the great Himalaya mountain range, to lay their eggs and raise their families. We have also discovered that many of the White Storks that visit us in winter are "Made in Germany"! The great hordes of Rosy Pastors that come to destroy our *jowar* crops in winter have travelled, many of them, all the way from Eastern Europe or Central Asia.

Unfortunately the war and the troubled conditions throughout the world have now put a stop to the international work of ringing birds. To produce successful results it is essential for this work to have the co-operation of all countries. Let us hope that the end of the war will bring a resumption of that friendly co-operation among the nations which proved so fruitful in the study of bird migration in past years.

5

The Monsoon Comes: Bird Life*

THE PIED CRESTED Cuckoo is a bird of distinguished look and unreticent demeanour. It bursts into our midst each year with clockwork regularity within the last three days of May or the first three of June, outriding the monsoon as it were. It proclaims its arrival by flying ostentatiously from tree to tree and calling noisily – a rather plaintive and metallic *piu . . . piu . . . pee-pee-pia . . . pee-pee-piu.*

Being of striking appearance and loud manners, it seldom fails to catch the eye of even such people as are normally not interested in a bird beyond whether it is better roasted or grilled. But the urban crow population is always far ahead of its human brethren in discovering a new arrival. The welcome they extend to it is unfailingly warm, in fact it may be more correctly presented as hot. With accustomed vulgarity and studied callousness they chivvy and chase the visitor about, shouting names and threats at it. They drive it to distraction, and the newcomer is indeed lucky if it manages to escape lynching by the villainous rabble.

* 29 June 1946, Bombay.

Every year at this period one gets reports from here, there, and eveywhere of these cuckoos being captured in rooms of dwelling houses and business offices, in the suburbs as well as in congested city localities where they have rushed in to escape their tormentors. And indeed this is how the Pied Crested Cuckoo is most often thrust on the unwilling notice of many people.

The ceaseless pestering of defenceless birds, and the robbing of their eggs and young, constitutes a serious charge against the crow in our towns and cities, with particular reference to this foremost city of India wherein we live. If I had the management of affairs, I would wage a holy war against the crow and liquidate it by every means at my command at least from within municipal limits, and in the shortest possible time. By this means alone can we hope to attract and encourage other more interesting, more beautiful, and more sweetly singing birds to the neighbourhood of our homes and gardens, and to shrubberies on vacant plots. As long as the crow is allowed to have the upper hand, as now, nothing else will have a chance to thrive. The argument invariably put forward by our City Fathers in defence of the crow within urban limits, is that it is a useful scavenger. So it is, and there is no denying the fact. Also it believes in no trade unions and never goes on strike which is perhaps another distinct advantage in these strife-ridden days. But it is open to question whether in modern times, and in this modern city which is not backward to call itself the foremost in India, the help of the crow is so indispensable to the city's sanitation. Is, or should, our Municipal Corporation be so completely dependent upon the good offices of the crow? We take a great deal of pride and trouble in planting beautiful flowering trees along our roadsides and in our public gardens and places. We could double the joys of beautiful flowers by adding beautiful birds to our surroundings. This should be tried, and it can be done, but not until the crow is shown its place.

That was a digression which is perhaps somewhat out of place in a talk like this, but it is a subject that must be close to the heart of every bird-lover. The crow has a direct bearing upon our bird life at any time, but particularly so during the monsoon when it is bringing up a family and wants food and more food for its young, and when there are marked incursions of beautiful and interesting birds from outside, defenceless enough to supply its wants.

And now to return to the Pied Crested Cuckoo. The regularity of its yearly arrivals in the Bombay area, and in many other parts of the country, is typical of the vast local migration or "general post-May" that takes place among birds at the onset of the monsoon. It represents just one of the many activities the monsoon sets in motion in the world of birds. There is so much interest in connection with the Pied Crested Cuckoo, and so much that we have still to learn about its life history, that despite the title of this talk it might be more profitable to confine myself mainly to it.

As many will know, the Pied Crested Cuckoo is a bird of about the size of the Myna with a much longer tail in proportion. This helps to give it its slim and elegant lines. In colour it is black above, white below. It has a roundish white patch on each of the black wings, and white tips to its black tail, both of which features are particularly conspicuous in flight. A prominent crest heightens its resemblance to an oversize bulbul. It belongs to the group of cuckoos known as Parasitic, notorious for their habit of laying their eggs in the nests of other birds. They shirk their parental responsibilities by foisting upon the dupes the bother of hatching their eggs and rearing their young. Our bird lays principally in the nests of Babblers, or Seven Sisters, whose pale blue eggs match its own, and who therefore presumably accept the impost without undue suspicion.

A thing of particular interest in regard to the monsoon movements of the Pied Crested Cuckoo is that simultaneously and just about the same time, i.e. immediately before the monsoon sets in, the species spreads out more or less over the entire Indian peninsula. And during this season two separate races of the bird are found: a larger confined to North India roughly above the latitude of Bombay, and a smaller – normally a resident of Ceylon and South India – which spreads northwards, riding on the wing of the monsoon, as it were, to meet the boundary of the larger form.

Now, the curious fact is that the larger race is not known to residents in India at all. It is never seen within our limits except during the monsoon. It is conjectured from purely circumstantial evidence that this larger race is migratory to and from Africa, where it is known to be present in winter. It has been claimed that the bird even breeds in Africa, laying a *white* egg there, as it lays a blue one here, in order to match the eggs of its local fosterers; but this is probably a mistake.

Whatever that may be, it just serves to show up our ignorance of many seemingly quite simple problems connected with the life of birds. Inspite of the great advances the science of ornithology has made in certain directions, our knowledge of many simple matters is as yet incomplete. The only evidence we possess that the African bird and the larger Indian race are one and the same is that both the birds are identical not only in measurements but also in every other detail. The normal condition with birds is that if two populations of the same species are isolated from each other by natural barriers – such as impassable mountain chains or wide stretches of ocean – they tend to develop divergences, as a result of peculiarities in their environments, which in course of time become established and emphasised, and serve as distinguishing marks between the members of the two populations. These are then termed geographical races of the species. In the African and North Indian cuckoos not only are there *no* distinguishing marks of this sort, but it is observed that the former is actually absent from Africa in the season that corresponds to our monsoon. The North Indian bird in turn, is absent from India at all seasons other than the monsoon! It is strange that notwithstanding the high probability of the correctness of our surmise, no specimens of this cuckoo have ever been taken on migration either in the Arabian Sea or on the mainland of Arabia over which its route must presumably lie.

The only method by which this mystery can be finally solved is by marking a large number of young Pied Crested Cuckoos while still in their foster parents' nests in North India, so that their subsequent movements can be definitely recorded. As many of you are probably aware, the modern method of marking birds with metal rings or bands is the one that is now widely employed to study their migrations, and also other matters connected with the lives of individual birds – such for instance as the age to which they live. The method consists in attaching an aluminium ring of appropriate size to the leg of a bird, either a nestling or one that has been trapped or netted. The ring bears on it a serial number and the address of the ringer. After marking, the bird is set at liberty. If at any time later on – it may be even as much as twenty-five years or more – this bird is killed or happens to be recovered in some other way, the particulars on the ring are communicated to the ringer who makes a record in his special register against the previous entry. When a large number of such recoveries are obtained, it is possible to piece together a great deal of useful information concerning the species which it would be impossible to obtain reliably in any other way.

If any of my listeners has kept notes about the dates and movements and habits of the Pied Crested Cuckoo in his or her area, I shall be happy if they will send them to me, or to the Bombay Natural History Society who have for some time been trying to unravel the problem of this bird's movements.

6

The Alien Migrants*

When I talk of alien migrants I am referring only to such birds as visit India from countries beyond our political frontiers – the true foreigners. In other words, such birds as would need valid passports and visas had they the doubtful privilege of being human. Apart from this class of long-distance migrants we have, of course, a constant traffic to and fro of local migrants – true nationals of India as it were – who move about freely with the seasons from one part of the country to another in search of better living.

Even the least birdy amongst us must be familiar with the topic of bird migration, at least with the name. The clockwork regularity with which the arrivals and departures of migratory birds take place every year, the countless millions of individuals involved in these mass movements, and the vast distances they travel over trackless land and sea to reach their seasonal goals, have excited the wonderment of Man through the ages. The influx into India from across our northern borders, which commences as a trickle in August, develops into a mighty flood-tide by the middle or end of October which overruns the entire subcontinent, sending out its tentacles into the remotest corners of the land, and partly spilling over into Ceylon.

*6 August 1957, Bombay.

Of the 1500-odd species of birds that figure on the Indian list, perhaps 25 per cent to 30 per cent constitute the true aliens of this class, who visit us only for the winter in order to escape the inhospitable conditions in their own homelands. They include birds of widely different families and of all shapes and sizes, from tall cranes and storks, standing almost the height of a man, and squat pelicans weighing up to 25 lb., to tiny delicate warblers not much larger than a thumb and weighing less than an ounce. The greatest part of the visual migration in and out of the Indian subcontinent is concentrated through our north-western and north-eastern frontiers – through the gaps in the Himalayan chain created by the Indus and Brahmaputra rivers. Nevertheless considerable movement also occurs directly across the entire length of the mountain barrier. Over this wide front it is more scattered and therefore less spectacular. Mountaineers have repeatedly recorded geese, duck, and cranes, as well as much smaller migratory birds, flying over some of the highest portions of the Karakoram and Himalayan ranges which they could easily have avoided by slight diversions if high flying really constituted a serious hazard for them. The first Everest Expedition found curlews, sandpipers, wagtails, pipits, and house martins passing over at 17,000 ft, and in Sikkim migrants regularly use some of the high passes like Nathu La as flyways. Except for sudden violent storms and blizzards which occasionally overtake these trans-Himalayan travellers and cause great mortality, the journeys are accomplished successfully and without undue losses. They help to shorten the journeys considerably than along the winding river valleys. With an astronomical telescope migrating wild geese have been identified at Dehra Dun flying across the face of the full moon at a calculated height of over five miles. Normally, however, most species fly under 3000 ft from the ground, and many only a few hundred feet above. When flying over the open sea birds prefer to fly low, often so close to the waves that they appear to be skimming them. Within the last thirty years or so we in India have been able, by means of the universally employed technique of marking birds with numbered and addressed aluminium rings, or bands round their legs, to determine the exact localities from which some of our alien visitors are derived, the routes by which they travel, and many other details of their journeys which before had been matters of mere conjecture and speculation. That at least some of the White Storks that visit India during the winter months come from Western Europe was proved by an individual marked as a nestling in Braunschweig in W. Germany on 11 June 1930, the desiccated remains of which were accidentally discovered lying on the margin of a tank in Bikaner in November of the same year. The ring was sent by the finder to the Bombay Natural History Society who procured the relative information from the Heligoland Bird Observatory whose address the ring bore. The time between ringing and recovery of this stork was just over five months, and the straight-line distance to Bikaner across the Caspian Sea about 3500 miles. A Green Sandpiper, a wading bird about the size of a myna and weighing scarcely 5 oz., ringed near Moscow in the USSR, was killed near Kottayam in South India, an air line distance of over 4000 miles. No political significance need be read into this record of a Russian bird arriving in Kerala! We have now collected a sufficient number of recoveries of Indian ringed ducks in Siberia, and of Russian ringed ducks in India, to show that the majority, if not all, of the migratory ducks that visit us in winter have their home or breeding grounds in Russia, up to 2500 miles away or more. Which means of course that all these alien visitors must travel double this distance each year, to and from their winter quarters. Another important record is that of the Rosy Starling or Tilyer, ringed in Eastern Hungary as a nestling and recovered a few months later in Lahore, 3000 miles away. Apart from the distinction of being one of the earliest migrants to arrive in India each year – numbers being already back from their breeding grounds by the end of July – this starling is recognised as a bird of great economic importance. Its food, whilst in our country, unfortunately consists largely of ripening *jowar* and other cereal crops to which its enormous swarms often cause serious damage. But to be weighed against this is the significant fact that the breeding grounds of the Rosy Starling which lie in Turkestan, the Middle East, and eastern Europe shift locally from year to year to coincide with the breeding grounds of the Migratory Locust, the hoppers and adults of which provide the staple food for the hordes of the birds and their young throughout the nesting period. Thus in its homeland this starling maintains a very effective and continuous check upon the increase of these destructive insects, while swarms of the birds also follow the migratory scourge to keep up the massacre among them. Incidentally it is just in a case like the Rosy Starling's – where a bird is almost entirely harmful in one country and almost wholly beneficial in another – that the need for international conventions for its protection becomes evident. The importance of the International Committee for Bird Preservation, functioning through affiliated national committees, will thus be realised. The Indian National Section of the I.C.B.P., which functions at home as the Bird Wing of the Indian Board for Wild Life, has the responsibility of seeing to it that ill-informed short-sighted unilateral action is not taken to decimate the Rosy Starling during its sojourn in India.

Some of our best-known long-distance migrating families are the ducks, geese, and cranes, birds of prey – eagles, hawks, harriers, etc. – waders and shore birds, thrushes and willow-warblers. The last, which include diminutive frail-looking birds, many of them hardly half the size and weight of a house sparrow, strangely enough contain also some of our most astonishing travellers. One of the rarer of these willow-warblers, which has so far only been recorded within Indian limits at Kohima in the Naga Hills of Assam, *Phylloscopus trochilus yakutensis*, breeds in N. Russia and regularly migrates to Africa in autumn, 7000 miles away, and back again the same distance in spring. A close relation of this, the Arctic Willow Warbler (*Ph. borealis*) breeds in Finland and Lapland and winters, among other places, in SE. Asia from 4500 to 6500 miles away, being then found also in the Andaman Islands.

The question may be asked: How long do the birds take to cover these distances? Some revealing answers have been provided by the marking method in the case of individual birds. In the US a young Bluewinged Teal was recovered at a distancc of 3800 miles exactly a month after marking, which means an average daily hop of about 120 miles. A Lesser Yellowlegs, closely related to our wintering Redshank, ringed in eastern N. America was taken in the West Indies six days later, having flown the intervening distance of 1900 miles at an average speed of 316 miles a day. A Turnstone, another shore bird seen on our coasts in winter, did the 510 miles from Heligoland to N. France in twenty-five hours. Birds travel southward in autumn rather leisurely, but the movement is greatly accelerated in spring when they are journeying northward to their breeding grounds. The speed then increases as the goal is approached. Warblers, which do an average of 20 miles per day, are known to accelerate to 200 miles a day when near the breeding range. Most birds pause for rest and food on the way, and may sometimes be held up for several days by bad weather and other causes.

Some, like the Birds of Prey, show a definite tendency to migrate by day, others like finches and warblers by night. Ducks and shore birds migrate during clear nights as well as by day. The

Grey Quail, the only alien migrant among our true game birds, starts moving at dusk, travels all night, and drops to earth before sunrise in the morning, often in the most inhospitable spots.

Millions enter India from the NW in autumn. They are eagerly awaited by the populace all along their accustomed route, and large numbers are killed and netted for food. Were it not that the quail is a prolific breeder, with scant respect for family planning and all that, it would have become extinct long ago.

The greatest success of the ringing method has come from those migrants which are widely shot or netted for sport or food, for example the ducks. Compared with many European countries, and with the USA and USSR, the number of ducks ringed in India is infinitesimal. Yet our recoveries have been most encouraging – something like 2 per cent – and include many valuable long-distance records. All the definitive knowledge we now possess concerning the migrations of our non-resident ducks is based upon such recoveries. With birds other than those normally shot or netted, the warblers for example, it is to be expected that returns will be scanty, since they must needs be more or less accidental and fortuitous. But some of the ways in which even such birds do get recorded seem little short of miraculous. I will only mention the case of a European Cuckoo ringed as a nestling in its fosterer's nest near London by boys of the Eton College Natural History Society. A few months later this ring was returned by a Christian missionary in Central Africa. It appears that the bird had been shot with bow and arrow by an aborigine who, thinking the inscribed shining band on its leg to be some form of divine message, naturally ran for enlightenment to the nearest man of god, who lived a good two days' foot-journey away. The expectant finder's reaction to the missionary's mundane explanation is not recorded, but the ring thus returned proved an important find for science.

However, this happened some years ago. Since then "Darkest Africa" has become more sophisticated. They no longer bother to return the rings; they just add them to their own personal adornments.

7

Birds in Summer*

IT MIGHT BE WELL to explain at the outset that for the purpose of this talk "summer" is meant to cover that part of the year, say from April to October, when all or nearly all of our winter migrants have departed for their northern homes, and only the resident birds are left in our midst. Summer therefore includes both the dry-hot and the succeeding wet-hot, or monsoon, months of the year. The season may be said to commence largely with the flowering of certain characteristic trees, like the Silk Cotton and Coral, whose blaze of brilliant red, nectar-rich blossoms act as signpost and magnet to the thirsty bird population of the parched countryside. Paradoxically enough, most of our deciduous trees shed their leaves and sprout luxuriant emerald green foliage just at this time of the year when the earth seems most parched and too tired to provide the necessary moisture. In this and other ways our early summer corresponds with spring in northern latitudes. Among the many signs that focus the bird-watcher's attention on this process of change is the gradual but rapid disappearance of the winter birds, so conspicuous everywhere until a few weeks before, and the marked animation and restlessness among the resident bird population – song, chasing,

*10 June 1963, Bombay.

territorial rivalry and fighting, competition for nest holes in tree trunks and buildings, sorties to and fro with nest material, and so on.

There has been a monstrous explosion in the crow population of Bombay City and suburbs within recent years – surely a reflection on the municipal sanitation of a city that likes to call itself the first in India, *Urbs prima in Indis*. Despite, however, their unceasing persecution of inoffensive ornamental birds – the song of the Magpie Robin, the flutey calls of the Blackheaded Oriole, the mellow sibilant whistles of the Iora, and the merry tinkling warble of the Fantail Flycatcher may still commonly be heard in such of the fast-shrinking wooded gardens and compounds as survive in the city and suburbs. But to appreciate the true emotional impact of summer on our resident bird life, when courtship and territorial and nesting activities are imminent or in full swing, one must visit places like our enviable Kanheri Park at crack of dawn – or, in rainy weather, just as the sun first peeps out on a drizzly morning. For then the concert is in full voice, including some of our finest songsters – the Spotted Babbler, the Whitethroated Ground Thrush, maybe even the Shama and the Malabar Whistling Thrush – and always that wonderful mimic the Racket-tailed Drongo, a sort of relaying or rediffusion station for them all, who seems to take an impish delight in confounding his listeners and keeping them guessing. Besides the full-throated songs of all those top-class performers, there are other species contributing to the general excitement by their striking or melodious calls – the shrill crescendo shrieks of the Koel and Brainfever Bird (or *Papeeha*), the mellow gurgling of the Scimitar Babbler, and many more, against the constant background music provided by the *pokok-pokok-pokok* of the Large Green Barbet and the monotonous *tonk-tonk* of its smaller relative, the Coppersmith. In the hotter parts of the day the birds are largely silent and so may escape the notice of such as are not specially looking for them; but there is usually another burst of song before they retire for the night.

The total number of bird species recorded within the limits of Greater Bombay and the immediately adjoining scrub and foothills country on the mainland, is about 350. This includes the resident population as well as the regular winter visitors, occasional stragglers, and accidental strays. The regular migrants number about 150, with perhaps another 25 or so of the other transients. The migrants, large and small, comprise land birds such as eagles, swallows, and wagtails, and waterbirds such as wild ducks, sea-gulls, and terns. But our largest group of migrants, both numerically and in conspicuousness, is the shore- or wading birds – the sandpipers and their ilk – which come in many sizes to enliven our sea coast, tidal creeks, and mudflats during the winter months. Living in open places they are easy to observe, and their gradual decrease and final disappearance as summer advances is readily noticed even by people not specially given to watching birds. Thus, in summer, after all the migrants are gone, we are left with a basic core of some 175 resident species which may truly be called our summer birds. While many of these nest within our area – some surprisingly enough even within fairly congested city limits despite the menace of the crow and the din and bustle of traffic – a number nevertheless find the Bombay monsoon too wet for their liking and retire to drier country above the ghats – the Deccan Plateau – whence they return with their adolescent families after the worst of the rains is over. The Rufous-backed Shrike is a typical example of this group known as Local Migrants. In this way there is a good deal of movement constantly going on even amongst our resident birds. The Pied Crested Cuckoo, a conspicuous and pleasantly boisterous black-and-white bird about the size of a myna with a longer tail and bulbul-like crest, for example, is one that literally bursts in on us with, or just before, the first pre-monsoon showers. At the end of May or early June, even as the weather prophets are debating if it will be an early monsoon or a late one, numbers of these cuckoos are already reported from various parts of the city and suburbs blundering into houses for refuge from what may be called "vested interests", namely the local crows. These renegades are always on the lookout for any defenceless newcomer who can be tortured and murdered with impunity. The Pied Crested Cuckoo stays in our area till the beginning of November, taking time off to bring up, or rather cause to be brought up, its family. For, like the koel, the bird belongs to the group known as Parasitic Cuckoos which has developed the convenient though somewhat disreputable habit of building no nest of its own but foisting its domestic chores upon various unsuspecting dupes – in this case mainly babblers of the *Satbhai* fraternity. It lays its blue egg in the babbler's nest, which in appearance is almost indistinguishable from those of the host.

One puzzle in connection with the Pied Crested Cuckoo remains unsolved. In Ceylon and South India is found, throughout the year, a resident form of this cuckoo, which moves northward to an undetermined limit on the wings of the South West Monsoon, as it were, to occupy a large portion of peninsular India. There it meets, and intermingles with, a slightly larger but otherwise superficially identical race of the same species which reaches North India and Kashmir likewise only during the rainy season, but supposedly from Africa. The assumption about its African origin seems circumstantially correct, because when the bird disappears from North India after the rains, its southern population does not show any appreciable swelling or concentration, as should undoubtedly be the case if all northern birds merely shifted south in the off season. The puzzle can only be solved by large-scale ringing of the birds in India as well as in Africa where the same, or at any rate an indistinguishable, population occurs. Unless individual birds can be identified with certainty by means of their rings, it is impossible to form a correct idea of their movements and life history.

All this leads up to the intriguing question: Why are some birds obliged to emigrate from our country in summer when others of their kind, superficially quite like them, closely related, and also with more or less similar food and habits, can live here throughout the year and breed freely? The northern migratory races are often impossible to distinguish from the resident population in the field in winter. Usually they can be told in the hand only by their slightly larger size and weight, and by the possession of longer and more pointed wings, better adapted for sustained migratory flight. It is a rule in nature that warm-blooded animals in the northern hemisphere – whether mammal or bird – grow progressively larger as they range from the equator to the pole. This is explained by the fact that absolute larger body size offers a relatively smaller surface and is thus better adapted for conserving body heat in cold climates. In the case of our resident birds, in the tropics, the condition is reversed: their smaller absolute body size with a proportionately larger surface area is a delicately adjusted temperature-control adaptation brought about by Natural Selection. In addition to the relatively larger heat-dissipating surfaces, the resident birds of the tropics possess a thinner feather covering, and for the same reason. An extreme example of this principle may be seen in the mutant breed of domestic poultry known as Frizzled-plumaged. These fowls have the feathers set up on end, allowing free escape of body heat. The birds are thus especially adapted to live under tropical conditions. In Europe they need to be kept in heated rooms in winter, otherwise they succumb to the cold.

8

The Migration of Birds*

EVEN PEOPLE WHO may know practically nothing about birds, except perhaps that some are good to eat, usually do have some vague, often fanciful notions about bird migration. The clockwork regularity of the annual migration of birds has been a cause of wonderment to man through the ages; it was well known to the ancient dwellers of the far northern lands, the fur-hunting Eskimos who named their calendar months after the comings and goings of the more familiar species. Yet the phenomenon of migration is not a speciality of birds alone, though it is most clearly noticeable among this class of animals. Seasonal movements of this kind are common to all animals, from mammals down to insects and the lower invertebrates.

The basic reason why birds and other animals migrate is, of course, self-evident. For birds living in the high north, around the Arctic Circle, let us say, life conditions become impossible in winter due to the extreme low temperatures, with consequent dwindling of the food supply – animal as well as plant items – when snow and ice cover the ground and all water sources are frozen. The shortage of food coupled with shortening hours of daylight for feeding forces the birds to move to lower and warmer latitudes

*15 January 1980, Poona.

nearer the equator, or perish. Thus, migration essentially involves changes in latitude. In the northern hemisphere the direction of the movement is broadly North and South, but there is evidence that the standard direction may differ in successive stages of a migratory journey.

Storms, especially when crossing sea or high mountains such as the Himalayas, often bring disaster. Strong cross-winds and fog when flying without landmarks, as over the ocean, may cause heavy lateral drift, sometimes carrying migrants off course to abnormal destinations. Drift can be corrected when visual landmarks are available but otherwise how correction is effected is open to question.

Fundamentally therefore it is the quest for food that compels birds to migrate, and this compulsion persists in varying degrees even in less harsh environments than the extreme north. With the return of warmer weather in spring and the resurgence of plant and animal life, coupled with longer hours of daylight for feeding and abundance of food – insects, berries, etc. – for themselves and their prospective progeny, and availability of uncrowded nesting sites, the process of migration is reversed. The birds return to the northern areas which in fact are their real home and which they were temporarily forced to abandon. In inter-tropical regions migrations are chiefly influenced by the rhythmic succession of wet and dry seasons which profoundly affect animals and plants, and thus the food supply – hatching of insects, ripening of fruit, etc. This is perhaps an oversimplification of an extremely complex natural phenomenon whose ramifications have continued to mystify and baffle human understanding for all time. Great advances have, however, been achieved in bird migration study in recent years by ingenious experimentation and with the aid of sophisticated technological devices such as radar, radio tracking or telemetry, and electronic computers. Nevertheless, some of the fundamental questions remain unanswered and seem unlikely ever to emerge beyond the realm of conjecture. Two of the many such stock questions almost invariably asked are: How do migrant birds know when to go and where to go, and what routes they must fly? And, how do they recognise the goal once they have arrived, considering that many are young birds of the year travelling for the first time in their lives, without previous experience, and often without guidance from their elders? No rational explanation for this can be given except the all too easy one of an "innate instinct" inherited through countless generations of migrants. This is the same sort of Inherited Instinct that, for example, impels a baya weaver bird, hatched out in an incubator and hand-reared – who has never seen its parents nor the nest in which their eggs were laid, yet begins at the appointed time and with no previous learning, to build the identical pattern of intricately woven nest that is characteristic of the species.

In addition to visual observation with telescopes, binoculars, etc., the most widely and internationally employed method nowadays of collecting basic factual information concerning bird migration is by ringing or banding the birds. This method consists of capturing wild birds in nets or traps and fixing a metal ring of appropriate size usually of aluminium or some light alloy round their legs. The ring bears the address of the ringer and a serial number which is entered on a registration card or form along with the bird's biodata, as it were – its species, sex, date and locality of ringing, age, weight, measurements, moult, and other relevant particulars. The bird is then released. If this bird is subsequently recovered dead or alive, the ring number, date and place of recovery, and other details are communicated to the ringer for the necessary recording. When a large number of such individual recoveries are plotted on maps and studied, or maybe computerised, they tell us a great deal in a way that no other can about the spatial movements of the species and other facets of the life history of individual birds, such as their longevity, faithfulness to breeding and wintering grounds, distances travelled, regularity and punctuality of arrivals and departures, and so on. In many countries of the world there are now nationally recognised bird ringing or banding centres that have their own ring markings. All ringers in their respective countries are urged to use only their national rings so as to promote co-ordination and to avoid wastage and dissipation of effort, as would be the case if every individual ringer were to use his private markings on the rings. The normal practice is for the national centres to issue their self-addressed rings only to recognised scientific institutions and competent bird students. In the U.K., aspiring bird ringers are required to pass a test of proficiency in identifying different species and in the handling of live birds before a ringing permit and rings are issued to them. In India, the Bombay Natural History Society and the Zoological Survey of India are the only two institutions that function as national ringing centres and who issue their rings only to approved bird students. All completed ring records are deposited with and studied at these institutions, and reports are published periodically in the *Journal of the Bombay Natural History Society.*

While migrating, some species, such as the Birds of Prey, fly singly, others like geese in small coalesced family parties, and others still like Rosy Starlings and shore birds in large compact flocks. Cranes, geese, ducks, and many others travel in orderly wedge-shaped formations or echelons headed by a leader who keeps changing places with other experienced adults. Some migrants prefer to fly by day while others do so at night. The day-flying ones are believed to navigate by the angle the sun makes with the earth and seem able to correct their bearings by means of an in-built time clock. Ingenious experiments have suggested that the night fliers are similarly guided in their course by the stellar constellations in the same way as the ancient mariners were, and primitive seafarers still are. Migrations of birds often cover distances of several thousand kilometres each way, between their summer home and their winter quarters. Land birds normally perform the journeys in successive stages often with halts of several days in between. Each stage may be from 200 to 400 miles, depending on the species of bird and the prevailing weather conditions. But enormous non-stop flights of, maybe, from 1500 to 3000 km and more may be accomplished while crossing the open ocean, sometimes requiring continuous flight of fifty to sixty hours without food or rest. An extreme and classical example is the Golden Plover – a species of shore bird which also winters in India – which flies from the Bering Sea area of extreme north-eastern Asia to the Hawaii islands, over 3000 km of open sea, apparently non-stop.

Of the 2000 odd species and subspecies of birds found in the Indian subcontinent about 300, or say 15 per cent, are winter visitors to the area. They come chiefly from the Himalayas and the countries beyond, that is, from Central and Northern Asia. Till fairly recently it was believed that their principal migration routes were the valleys of our great northern rivers – the Indus and the Brahmaputra and their tributaries – which provided easier access than over the lofty Himalayan barrier. However, increasing evidence to the contrary is gathering from visual observations of mountaineers and the frequent finding of remains of dead birds at great height which obviously perished in storms and blizzards while flying over the mountain range. These circumstances suggest that a considerable amount of migration must also take place directly across the mountains. Moreover, contrary to previously held notions concerning the ceiling-potential of migratory flight, radar has now disclosed that even small frail-looking birds often travel at up to 20,000 feet and more, although there is no apparent compulsion for them to do so, and obviously without physical discomfort. A direct Himalayan crossing would actually be a distinct advantage to the bird by reducing the distance and time and also its expenditure of energy, though at the same time perhaps increasing the hazard of occasional misadventure.

Since 1960 the Bombay Natural History Society has been particularly active in the study of bird migration problems in India. Close on 300,000 birds have so far been ringed, of which several thousand have been recovered in distant lands. In this way a great deal of original scientific data has accumulated which is being analysed and processed for interpretation. It is proposed to expand and intensify the migration research over the next five years by a comprehensive network of field stations covering all the diverse environments throughout the country.

PART III

LEARNING ABOUT BIRDS

"Recognising birds in the field with tolerable accuracy is in essence like learning the alphabet. It is the essential minimum qualification for the proper intellectual and aesthetic enjoyment of birds, and for making useful contributions to scientific knowledge"

– Sálim Ali, Radio Talks, "Trends in Modern Bird Study" (1955)

Examining a florican with researchers and Forest Dept staff.
Madhya Pradesh, 1985.
(*Photo by Asad Rahmani*)

With his student, measuring an abnormally long Baya nest,
Poona 1958.

1

Birds

A National Asset*

IT IS VERY TRUE that we seldom appreciate a blessing until we have lost it. Fortunately for us, the blessing of India's prolific bird life – certainly one of her major natural and national assets – is not yet lost, but this may well happen in the case of many useful and beautiful species if the present attitude of apathy or of wanton and unceasing persecution is persisted in. Those who indulge in this attitude will be the loudest to moan when their fell handiwork is accomplished. Indeed they are the loudest to moan even today while they pursue their vandalism with unabated recklessness, that bird life is no longer what it was say thirty, twenty, or even ten years ago.

The fact is that inspite of statutory closed seasons and other theoretical forms of protection accorded to certain species of birds, the position in many parts of the country remains far from satisfactory. No laws, however beneficial and well-intentioned they may be, can function effectively unless they are backed by public opinion. The lack of educated public opinion is the most important factor that makes bird protection measures in India so

*2 December 1941. Broadcast from Lahore.

largely inoperative. The schools are the cradle of public opinion, and the fault lies with our system of schooling. It is deplorable that so little attention is paid to the teaching of natural history in Indian schools. No effort worth the name is made to arouse in schoolchildren an active interest in Nature or to make them understand and appreciate the great natural heritage that is theirs. Children who give any attention to animals at all are those with catapults and airguns who mostly grow up with no other outlook on living creatures than as objects to destroy for pleasure. And of course in later life if such killing results in monetary gain, a further incentive is provided for more wholesale destruction.

The national economic importance of our bird life is seldom recognised. Yet its influence is exerted on almost every branch of human activity, though it may not always be direct or obvious. But the strength of a chain is in its weakest link; birds constitute a link in a great many chains of human life and industry which is by no means always the weakest. To give an example: few realise how greatly responsible birds are for the success of the present-day match industry in India. The wood of the Silk Cotton tree or Simal (*Bombax malabaricum*) has been found to be the most satisfactory for match manufacture. It is soft and of a suitable quality; it grows abundantly and all over the country which makes its extraction and transport easy. The large showy crimson flowers of this tree, doubtless familiar to most people, contain a plentiful supply of sugary nectar which is eagerly sought and greedily eaten by birds of numerous species. In trying to reach the nectar the ripe pollen-dust brushes on to the feathers of the forehead and throat and is transported to the female parts of the next flower visited, which it fertilises. Birds thus contribute to the production of fertile seed. They ensure the continuance of healthy generations of the tree, and incidentally the supply of raw material for your box of matches. Investigations reveal that we are ultimately dependent upon birds in this house-that-Jack-built sort of way for a great many of our everyday necessities. Like bees and other insects, birds of diverse families are responsible for the cross-pollination of a large variety of flowers, some of which are so highly specialised in shape and structure that they cannot be fertilised by any other agency. The large part they play in this capacity has been consistently underestimated.

Birds act a predominant role in the dissemination of seed and the distribution of the plant life of this country. Bulbuls, barbets, and a wide variety of frugivorous birds greedily devour the berries of numerous plant species. The seeds pass through the bird's intestine uninjured, or even improved, by the digestive juices. They germinate rapidly under favourable conditions of soil and climate and establish themselves. The abundance of sandalwood trees in parts of southern India is largely due to seeds dispersed in this way, and one has only to look at the flourishing abundance of mulberry trees in the newly colonised canal areas in this province to appreciate the importance of birds in seed dispersal.

But perhaps the most important item of birds' usefulness is the constant and rigid check they maintain on the over-increase of insect pests, and of rats, mice, and similar vermin.

The voracity and fecundity of insects is phenomenal. There are over 30,000 forms described from the Indian Empire, the majority of which are harmful to crops, forestry, livestock, and other human interests. The Hop Aphis, very destructive to grass and cereals in America, would if allowed unchecked multiplication reach the astronomical figure of 10 sextillion individuals in less than a year. It has been calculated that if this brood were marshalled end to end at the rate of 10 per inch the procession would be so long that light, travelling at 184,000 miles per second, would take 2500 years to reach from end to end!

A caterpillar eats about twice its own weight in leaves per day. The food taken by a single silkworm in 56 days is 86,000 times its original weight at hatching. Locusts are as notorious for their prolific reproduction as for their prodigious appetites. An invasion from a swarm – which is often so thick as to obscure the sun – will, in the course of a few short hours, convert a green and smiling land into a desolate tract with nothing but bare stems standing. From the rate at which insects multiply it is clear that unless their numbers were kept under constant and strict control all vegetation would soon disappear from the face of the earth. There is much truth in the saying that all flesh is grass considering that green plants in one form or another comprise the prime source of food for all animals. Thus the disappearance of vegetation would mean the disappearance of all life on the globe.

An overwhelming proportion of the food of a very large proportion of birds consists of insects. Birds not only take a heavy toll of the marauding locust hordes all along their flight lines, but they also scratch up and devour their eggs in large quantities, as well as young locusts in all stages after hatching. The White Stork is a well-known locust destroyer, and enormous nesting colonies of the Rosy Pastor (also known as Jowari-bird or *Tilyer*) live and feed their young exclusively upon these insects on their common breeding grounds in Central Asia and Eastern Europe. Such birds as the Drongo or King-Crow (*Kotwāl* or *Kālkalachi*) and the Roller or Blue Jay (*Nilkant*), to mention two of our commonest species, invariably present about cultivation, are amongst the truest benefactors of the ryot. They wage unceasing war against his insect enemies and their benefactions are beyond computation. This warfare is waged not only when insects are at the peak of their periodic abundance, but it is incessant and relentless, and where they have not been unwisely interfered with birds constitute one of the most effective natural checks upon insect numbers. Digestion in birds is a rapid and continuous process; the weight of food consumed per day in relation to body weight is extraordinarily high, and it is this indeed that makes bird life such an indispensable balancing force in Nature.

Owls, Kestrels, Hawks, and the birds of prey generally keep down the numbers of rats and mice, some of the most fecund and destructive vermin from which Man and his works suffer. Besides devastating crops and agricultural produce they are the carriers, directly or indirectly, of diseases often fatal to Man. While on the one hand Man's crops and granaries provide easy and lavish sustenance to these destructive hordes, he on the other slays mercilessly and without discrimination every species of hawk and owl in the mistaken belief that he is thereby protecting his poultry and game from their ravages.

Vultures, Kites and Crows are invaluable as scavengers. With astounding speed and thoroughness they dispose of the carcasses of cattle and other garbage dumped in the precincts of our villages, notoriously lacking in modern sanitation, that would otherwise putrefy and befoul the air and produce veritable culture beds of disease. Their services are of special value during famines and cattle epidemics when large numbers of domestic animals perish and bestrew the countryside.

Quails, partridges, and other game birds are snared and netted for food, and innumerable other species are caught and sold in the bazaars to bird fanciers, bringing in substantial profits to those engaged in the trade. The netting operations carried on in the *jheels* of northern India during the winter months attain great proportions. Wildfowl of every description are supplied to the markets of the larger towns both near and distant. The population in the vicinity of these *jheels* subsists largely during the winter months on the flesh of waterbirds or on the traffic in them.

Until a few years ago egret-farming, for the sake of the dainty ornamental breeding plumes of the birds, was a lucrative cottage industry and largely practised on the *jheels* in Sind and other places in northern India. The feathers, exported mostly to Europe, for ladies' head-dresses, tippets, muffs, and boas were almost worth their weight in gold. But fickle is womankind and so are its fashions. With the change in vogue, egret feathers no longer carry the same demand: prices have dwindled and most of the once-flourishing farms have disappeared.

There are other minor products of birds which if properly husbanded could be made to yield considerable revenue in India. The saliva nests of the so-called Edible Swiftlets which breed in vast colonies on islands off the coasts of Burma and W. India, are even now the source of considerable income to those engaged in the trade and of royalty to Government. The nests, which look like tiny saucers of isinglass, are collected and exported to China for soups and other epicurean purposes. The better qualities fetch from Rs 7 to 14 per lb. and the value of nests imported into China in three recent years (prior to the "Incident") totalled some 25 lakhs of rupees. A fair proportion of them came from the Indian Empire.

The fertilising properties of Guano, the excrement of sea birds such as gannets, pelicans, and cormorants, are widely known wherever intensive agriculture is practised. It occurs in vast stratified accumulations on islands off the Peruvian coast in South America where these birds nest in unbelievable numbers. It is a product of great commercial value. Although the true guano birds are not found within our limits, yet in many localities we have shallow *jheels* on which thousands upon thousands of storks, cormorants, and other waterbirds nest. The fertilising properties of this water, which soon becomes a decoction of the birds' droppings, are fully appreciated by the local ryots, and there is no doubt that if systematically exploited this guano could be turned to good account.

From all that has been said it must not be assumed that our bird life is all asset and no liability. Indeed, birds are injurious to Man's concerns in a number of ways. At all times they raid his crops and damage his flower beds, orchards, and vegetable gardens; they sometimes act as intermediate hosts of parasites that spread diseases among his livestock, and carry them far and wide in the course of their wanderings; they propagate noxious plants and weeds; they often devour beneficial insects and prey upon fish and other animals used by Man as food. All this is true. But there can be no doubt that the good they do far outweighs the harm. Any toll they take must therefore be looked upon as no more than the labourers' hire – a sort of trade expense.

The case for the protection, conservation, and economic research of birds in a country like India, so largely agricultural and forested and therefore at their mercy, clearly requires no eloquent advocacy. Quite apart from the purely materialistic aspect of the matter, however – the aspect of rupees, annas, and pies – their great aesthetic value must not be lost sight of, and we must remember that Man cannot live by bread alone. By the gorgeousness of their plumages and the loveliness of their forms, by the vivaciousness of their movements, buoyancy of their flight, and the sweetness of their songs birds typify Life and Beauty. They rank beyond price, and are undoubtedly among those important trifles that supplement bread in the sustenance of Man and make his living worthwhile.

2

Bird Study in India*

I AM OFTEN ASKED by people who see me dawdling about in the countryside with a pair of binoculars hung round my neck, peering into bushes or shadowing the comings and goings of what seems to them a perfectly unremarkable looking bird, why I waste my time in this unprofitable pursuit. Indeed it is difficult to convince a certain type of person of the profit in any occupation unless you can show him some inherent possibilities of black marketing.

In the first talk of this series entitled "The Kingdom of Birds" my friend Dillon Ripley has told you of some of the marvels and mysteries of bird life. Among other things you have heard of the enormous journeys many birds perform twice each year in order to escape the rigours of winter and to enjoy the bounties of springtime. The regularity, punctuality, and precision with which these movements are carried out often over thousands of miles of land and sea, even by young birds without previous experience of the route or the goal, has excited the wonderment of man from earliest times.

While we have learnt a good deal about the migrations of birds in general, through the efforts and researches of bird students in

*19 July 1947, Bombay, for broadcast from Delhi.

Europe and America, it has to be admitted that in relation to India specifically our knowledge is still in a very elementary stage. This is also the stage at which we find ourselves as regards most other problems concerning the lives of Indian birds. What I want to impress upon listeners in the present talk is about the importance and value of bird study in India, particularly that part of it which concerns the living bird in its natural environment. Practically all that we know about Indian birds has been learnt during the last 125 years. And it has all come through the active interest taken in our bird life by a handful of Britishers. They were not imported especially as luxury articles in order to study our birds for us, but people who extracted opportunities from their governmental or professional duties, and devoted their leisure to the pursuit of their hobby. In other words they were all amateurs mostly. Through the piecemeal efforts of these men has been built up all the knowledge that we now possess of Indian birds.

The foundation has been well and truly laid and it is now up to us to design and erect a superstructure that will do credit to ourselves, and thereby also to the pioneers who provided the foundation. Of the many things that Britishers will be remembered by in years to come when distance in time enables us to form a truer perspective of their achievements and shortcomings, one will certainly be the contribution they have made to the study of Indian birds. It is a coincidence that may be news to many people that the same Allan Hume who was one of the founders of the Indian National Congress, and thus in a way the spiritual ancestor of the Quit India resolution, was also the virtual father of Indian ornithology. He encouraged bird collectors in every part of the country to send him specimens and from his official duties found time to edit a journal called *Stray Feathers*, the ten volumes of which, though now difficult to obtain, form an indispensable work of reference for every serious student of Indian birds.

In these few minutes I want to give you an outline of the work done by these pioneers; to tell you in fact how much we actually do know about Indian birds, and what we have still to learn.

The first concern of the earlier ornithologists was naturally to discover how many different kinds of birds were to be found within the boundaries of the Indian Empire as it then was. They themselves collected, and they caused to be collected through local shikaris and snarers, specimens in every corner of the country, the chief aim of every collector being no doubt to obtain something that nobody else had collected before, and which could be described as a species new to science. The chief ambition of most collectors even today, sometimes veiled, sometimes undisguised, is to discover a bird such as has never been seen or dreamt of. I myself sometimes feel that I would like to give to the world a pigmy owlet with a peacock's train! Most of these Indian collections sooner or later found their way to the British Museum, which, in spite of the recent acquisitions by some museums in the U.S.A., perhaps still contains the richest Indian material.

Some of these early collectors devoted themselves more specially to collecting birds' eggs. In their zeal to get eggs of a larger and larger number of species they often employed gangs of jungle tribes to collect for them, with rather unfortunate results. It was sometimes impossible to establish the identity of the birds that were described by the men who brought in the eggs, and errors have thus crept into ornithological literature which are difficult to eradicate.

However, the position is that through the united labours of all these volunteers we now know that the total number of species and sub-species of birds to be found in India is in the neighbourhood of 2400, of which about 500 visit the country only during the winter months. These latter do not nest in our midst. Regarding most of the residents – but yet not all – we know when they breed, what sort of nests they build, the number of eggs they lay, and what the shape, size, and colouration of their eggs are. But apart from these basic facts, there is little else that we can lay claim to. While all the attention has been centred in the collecting, naming, and describing of dead material, the living bird has been practically ignored. We really know exceedingly little, and that only scrappily, about the life histories of most species. And it is only in comparatively recent years that any attention has been given to this aspect of bird study. There was even a time not so long ago, when bird watching – the only possible way in which the living bird can be studied – was looked down upon by museum workers as a harmless enough but rather childish way of killing time. The observations of field naturalists were sometimes treated with condescending tolerance, but little scientific importance was attached to them. All this has given some people an idea that because they do not kill birds and stuff them and preserve their dry skins they are incapable of contributing anything seriously worthwhile to the study of birds. I can tell you that nothing is farther from the truth. The truth is that at the stage bird study has reached in India it is unnecessary, except in special areas and by specialists who know what they want, to go on collecting bird skins or eggs in a haphazard way any longer. The gun and the skinning knife must now give way to the binoculars and the notebook. We want to know exactly how birds live: why they select particular habitats, how the environment reacts on them, and how they react on their environment. What food birds eat, their preferences for different foods, and the quantities they consume. What determines and controls the density of bird populations in different areas. We want to know more of the social life of different species of birds, the interflock relationship of individuals, and the relations of one species with another. We want to know about their courtship displays and pair-formation rites, their attitudes towards their young, and their behaviour under unaccustomed circumstances. And we want to know about their different calls and emotions and reflexes. We want to learn more precisely about their migrations.

Now these are not things that can be studied in a musty museum from dry and shrivelled-up skins with the help of calipers and slide rules. They are things that you and I who watch birds intelligently enough to enjoy them can contribute to as we wander about the fields and hedgerows and jungles even while we enjoy the open air, the blue sky, and the song of the birds. All you need in the way of equipment is a good pair of binoculars, a notebook and a pencil, a good stock of patience, and a capacity to observe keenly and record faithfully. That is the sort of bird study of which we stand in the greatest need in India today, and for which we need recruits and more recruits in every part of the country.

3

Courtship and Display Among Birds*

THE SUBJECT OF courtship and display among birds is a branch of the much wider study of animal behaviour. It is easy to understand its popularity with both field ornithologist and aviculturist, i.e. the man who breeds and studies birds in captivity – since the bird in love indulges in the most extravagant and often fantastic antics and provides lavish material for a comparative study of the physiological and psychological processes that living creatures undergo in this exalted state. For it is not birds alone that behave extravagantly at the period which precedes breeding. All animals, from the lowliest in the scale to Man himself, show distinctly abnormal behaviour. The ridiculous spectacle of the young master in love is well recognised by all of us who do not themselves happen to be similarly afflicted for the moment!

The courtship and display of birds takes on a very special fascination on account of its appeal to our aesthetic sense by the ornamental plumes and showy appendages worn by the males of many species. These adornments are employed in a variety of ways to show off before the opposite sex and in the rites that precede

*6 September 1947, Bombay, for broadcast from Delhi.

mating. The performances are of great diversity and charm, and range in quality from the sublime to the ridiculous. But whatever their nature, they closely follow well-defined patterns in the case of related groups of birds. A critical study of courtship and display patterns has, in recent years, helped to rationalise the work of systematics and classification and to establish, confirm, or refute relationships between groups of birds hitherto assigned on less obvious or satisfactory considerations.

In those birds where the sexes differ in colouration, it is usually the male who is the more brilliantly coloured and showy. A familiar example of this is the peafowl. The well-known "dance" of the peacock, with his gorgeous train expanded and erected like a fan, strutting and posturing in front of a hen, is an obvious effort to show himself off at his best and to impress on her what a fine fellow he is. Frequently, several cocks will perform in this way before a single hen, each seemingly doing his utmost to please.

The theory of Sexual Selection, popular till not so long ago, purported to explain the purpose and origin of the brilliant plumage and showy adornments possessed by male birds like the peacock. It assumed that the sober-coloured females actively exercised selection of a mate from amongst a number of suitors displaying before them, favouring the one who possessed the most showy plumage or gave the most pleasing performance. In other words, this theory suggested that the female selected her mate by "Swayamvara" on the traditional Draupadi–Arjun pattern; that only the handsomest and most virile males were thus able to secure mates and produce offspring, while the less fit – failing to get partners – gradually got weeded out in the struggle for existence. Subsequent research has shown that the matter is perhaps not as simple as all that. It is observable that the female often pays not the slightest attention to the amorous antics of the cock or cocks before her. Also, it is not easy to account for the fact that a peacock will frequently go through all its elaborate courtship display when no female is present. He will sometimes even do so in front of an inanimate object that has touched his emotions, such as his feeding tray or a brick wall. The peacock is polygamous and maintains a regular harem in the breeding season. But even in birds that pair for life, such as cranes and eagles, where no fresh selection of mates takes place at the commencement of each breeding season, it is observed that the birds go through elaborate courtship ceremonials. To most people who have an eye for birds – or even merely for the strange and unusual – the fantastic courtship rites of the Sarus Crane in the early monsoon are probably not unfamiliar. Both birds of a pair indulge in wild and ludicrous prancing and capering, spreading out their great wings, bowing, and leaping in the air round each other. How would the Sexual Selection or "Swayamvara" theory account for such complicated displays in the case of birds already mated?

The theory of Territory in bird life was elaborated by Eliot Howard in the early years of the present century. It has completely revolutionised our outlook on this aspect of bird behaviour and helped to explain a number of puzzles. It is now recognised that the term "Display", originally used to signify what one may call the exhibitionism of the male with the object of making himself acceptable to the female, also includes movements, postures, and sounds which serve to bring about certain definite responses, particularly from members of the same species of both sexes. Therefore "Display" as at present understood connotes much that is not strictly connected with sex, though outwardly the actions may be the same as in courtship. It is perhaps necessary here to explain briefly the implications of the Territory theory. It works out somewhat as follows: On the approach of the breeding season, many male birds who have till then been living amicably in flocks of mixed sexes tend to separate. Individual males select some exposed or elevated perch and begin to sing. They have remained silent during the flocking period. The object of the song is to proclaim to all comers, especially to males of his own species, that he is "King of the Castle" and in occupation or an area around the singing post. In other words, it is a warning to other males to keep off. If this warning is disregarded, the interloper is first met with angry threats and posturings, often outwardly identical with courtship display. If this sabre-rattling fails to deter the rival, battle ensues in which feathers fly and one or the other of the combatants may even be killed. Apart from distant threat and warning of this nature, song discharges at the same time another important function. Considering the acuteness of the sense of hearing in birds, it is not unreasonable to assume that the song of the male is appreciated by the female, and that it attracts her and produces a physiologically stimulating effect upon her. Song does, in fact, achieve the purpose of the stereotyped matrimonial advertisement so popular in our daily newspapers, that "A young and handsome gentleman of dash dash community, well established in life (and perhaps even a Gazetted Officer!) would like to meet a beautiful and accomplished young lady of fair complexion, with a view to matrimony." In response to the song a suitable charmer duly arrives on the scene. After a good deal of playful chasing about, she pretending to resent his forwardness yet protesting too much the while, the female finally settles down and is accepted by the male as his wife. Once the female is secured and family responsibilities begin, the male tones down considerably and stops his singing and preventive displays. Encroachment of the Territory after this stage, either by an outside male or female, is actively resented by both owners. But elaborate ceremonials now follow, as between the mated pair, which may be considered true Courtship Display. This, as I have said, follows well-defined family patterns. Three main types of Courtship Display may be recognised:

(1) *Individual Display* in groups where the sexes differ considerably in appearance such as in the Peafowl
(2) *Mutual Display* in groups where the sexes are more or less identical to look at, e.g. Storks, Cranes, Parakeets, Pigeons, etc. Both sexes take part in the ceremonials equally, their actions producing a mutually stimulating effect
(3) *Communal Display* indulged in by birds such as Gulls and Terns that nest in large colonies. Here the rituals started by one member of a colony, either male or female, who is physiologically readier to breed than the rest, has an infectious effect upon the others (of both sexes) and results in mass display. This promotes the hastening of egg-laying and other activities within the colony and conduces in a number of ways towards successful reproduction.

There isn't time enough today to describe the varied and fascinating courtship displays of any Indian birds specifically. There is one, however, which many of my listeners should doubtless have opportunities of witnessing. If the opportunity occurs I commend you to spend a half hour observing and noting the comical goings on of a pair of Rose-ringed Parakeets. These birds are common enough in the plains everywhere and they nest freely in holes in walls, even of occupied houses, and often in the midst of noisy bazaars. It is a performance of great interest and extreme ludicrousness and will amply repay your watching.

In a recent broadcast on Bird Study in India, I drew attention to the various aspects of Indian bird life about which our knowledge is woefully meagre. One of these, it may be recalled, was Courtship and Display. It is a subject to which every intelligent birdwatcher can contribute, since we have to begin almost from scratch. Apart from a rather diffuse and general understanding of the ways of only some of our commoner birds, we know practically nothing about this important chapter in the life history of most of our species.

To those interested in the subject and wanting to learn more about it, I can recommend no better book than that by E.A. Armstrong entitled *Bird Display: An Introduction to the Study of Bird Psychology* published by the Cambridge University Press in 1942. It is a particularly lucid and well-written account, and an epitome of all the more important researches of recent years.

4

How I Became Interested in Birds*

As an Indian ornithologist, one of the questions I have repeatedly to answer is how my interest in birds first began and what makes me continue in the quest of birds considering that the majority of them are uneatable – or at any rate too tiny to make their eating worthwhile!

Well, as far as I can now recall it all started quite accidentally when I was about nine, when like the majority of unspeakable little urchins I was at the murderous airgun stage. But in my own case it must be pleaded that owing to the somewhat innocuous nature of my weapon and the lack of expertness in its handling, birds were as a rule pretty safe.

On one of my rare occasions of successful murder I noticed that the victim, which was intended to be a common House Sparrow, bore a curious yellow patch on the throat, rather like the impression left by a curry-stained thumb. When the bird was carried home in triumph, none of my elders could account for this mysterious yellow patch, but I was encouraged to seek enlightenment from the museum of the Bombay Natural History Society. My first visit to this museum, which has now almost

*15 March 1950, Singapore.

become a second home to me, was a memorable and rather terrifying experience. Stuffed heads of tigers, leopards, bears, and other carnivores snarled ferociously down at one from the walls. One had to steer carefully to avoid stumbling over stuffed crocodiles and assorted skulls and skeletons of other monsters which littered the floor, or bumping into glass cases containing live pythons and cobras which adorned the various nooks and corners. Through the kindly interest of the Society's Secretary I had the pride and satisfaction of being shown over the museum cabinets of made-up bird skins from all parts of the country and of identifying my enigmatic bird as the Yellow-throated Sparrow, a common species found over most of the Indian peninsula. I think it was here that I first became consciously aware of the fact that there existed many other kinds of sparrow besides the species specially created to be a nuisance to us in our houses. It aroused in me a sort of ambition to find out as much as possible about as many kinds of sparrows as were to be seen in India by reading up all I could about them and collecting specimens of as many different kinds as I came across.

In course of time the field naturally enlarged itself to include other birds as well. From birds to their eggs was a natural step, and so it went from egg-collecting to a study of nesting habits, and to the ways in which birds live, their adaptation to their environment, and also to bird photography. Thus, like ripples from a pebble dropped in water, the circles of my interest in ornithology widened.

While this is the genesis of my interest in birds I cannot claim to attribute the fact of its having endured and gathered momentum during the years to anything loftier or more noble than self-indulgence. As a boy it was far pleasanter to be chasing birds than doing ridiculous sums in elementary mensuration. Since then I have watched and studied birds largely for the pleasure and satisfaction they give me, and for the opportunities their pursuit provides of removing myself to pleasant places for long periods of time – away from the newspaper, the radio, and the telephone, and all the ghoulish appurtenances that savour of the doubtful civilisation of this mechanical high-speed age. Admittedly this is a form of escapism, but one for which the world today furnishes ample justification.

But I must also say here that my pleasure in studying birds does not derive entirely from this source, nor is it sustained wholly by the escapist motive. The possibility of making a contribution to scientific knowledge by careful recording and interpretation of data collected in the field bearing on some knotty problem of animal behaviour or evolution is one of the carrots that are forever dangling in front of the persevering ornithologist.

While the chances of discovering anything startlingly new in the way of bird species are no longer within the bounds of probability, considering the amount of exploration that has been carried out in most parts of the world, yet they are not remote enough to be entirely out of the thoughts of the field ornithologist working off the beaten track. The romantic search for and discovery of the brand-new peacock-like bird Afropavo in the forests of Belgian Congo within the last few years, and the recent finding in New Zealand of living examples of the flightless bird Notornis believed to be long extinct, show that the age of wonders is not past and provide just the needed fillip to the jaded hopes of the seeker after undiscovered birds.

Most of my ornithological work relates to Indian birds and may not be of any direct significance to bird students in this country. But there is one aspect of it which should interest listeners in Malaya. This problem of bird geography first drew my attention in 1930 while engaged on a survey of the bird life of Travancore. Since then I have had opportunities of working at it off and on and been able to amass a considerable amount of suggestive evidence leading to conclusions of a highly satisfying character. Briefly stated, this problem concerns the close parallelism, also remarked upon by previous investigators, that exists between the flora and fauna of Ceylon together with the extreme south-western corner of peninsular India on the one hand, and of the Eastern Himalayas, Assam, Yunnan, Burma, and the Malay Peninsula and islands on the other. Certain families, genera, and species of birds, of which the Great Pied Hornbill, the Fairy Bluebird, the Great Eared Nightjar, the Trogons, Frogmouths, Laughing Thrushes, and Bazas may be cited as some of the more outstanding examples, are found living in the humid evergreen rain forests of these far-flung areas sundered from their nearest populations by a gap of 1500 miles or more of country totally unsuitable for their existence. Our problem was to provide an explanation for the enormous spatial gap that now separates the two populations. Methodical collecting of bird specimens in the intervening blank areas and collation of carefully recorded ecological data over many years in different parts of the country led to the suggestion that at one stage in the geological history of the Indian peninsula there must have existed a continuous chain of high hilly country with the necessary humid climatic and physiographical conditions, and that these Indo-Malayan birds must then have had an unbroken distribution from one end of their present overall range to the other. Geological evidence has now come to light showing that the Satpura range of mountains which stretches right across the middle of peninsular India from west to east once stood at least 3000 ft higher than it is today – a condition that would provide the humid environment necessary for the existence of these specialised forms of birds. The north-eastern extremity of the Satpuras was connected with the Himalayas, possibly through the Garo Hills of Assam, serving as a bridge for the fauna and flora. Weathering and erosion operating over tens of thousands of years has worn the Satpuras down to their present levels, but some of the specialised humid forest birds still persist in relict enclaves of the required humidity and vegetation at the higher elevations all along this mountain trend.

The evidence supplied by my studies of bird life is fully corroborated by the results of the researches of eminent Indian scientists working quite independently on the freshwater fish fauna of torrential hill streams. Significantly enough the specialised fish faunas of the two regions above mentioned also show parallelisms of an identical nature as regards the distribution of genera and species. Since this group of fishes is narrowly adapted for a life in torrential streams and incapable of thriving in placid waters, their distribution in space necessarily depends entirely upon interconnection at one period or another of all the hill streams in which they now occur. The curious distribution of closely related torrential fishes today provides perhaps the most convincing confirmation of the ornithological evidence that there was once a continuous mountain connection between Malaysia and the Travancore/Ceylon region by way of the Eastern Himalayas and the Satpura trend. Large sections of this highway have now disappeared in the middle, leaving marooned populations at its south-western end, and in enclaves all along the trend. This explanation of the discontinuous distribution of Indo-Malayan plants and animals is gradually gaining general acceptance by Indian biologists and zoogeographers. It has come to be known as the Satpura Hypothesis and workers in other fields of zoology are steadily adding evidence in its support.

Short though my present visit to Singapore has been, it has helped to furnish me with a very good general picture of the climate, vegetation, and natural conditions under which birds live at this, the eastern extremity of what we call the Indo-Malayan "arc" or "horseshoe" of animal distribution.

But as I mentioned earlier on, one of my particular interests lies also in studying the ecology of birds – their nesting habits and their adaptations to their native environment. Therefore, I never lose an opportunity of visiting my friends in their distant homelands at the appropriate season in order to complete my circuit of their life histories. The quest has led me to far-flung corners of the earth. I have followed the Bar-headed Goose to its native lakes on the bleak Tibetan highlands, and have now successfully tracked down Loke Wan Tho to the lush pasture meadows of Cathay in the heart of Singapore city. And the forthcoming International Ornithological Congress in Sweden will, I hope, enable me to follow our Godwits and some of our rarer migratory wading birds to their nesting marshes in Lapland – the Land of the Midnight Sun.

5

Answering Questions about Birds*

IN TODAY'S TALK I am going to answer some of the questions that are commonly put to me at the end of my lectures on birds by persons who, though not birdwatchers themselves, are sufficiently interested to want to know about their ways and habits. Many of these questions are of such frequent recurrence that they point to the broad lines along which popular interest in birds runs in the mind of what one may call the man in the street. It may be that many listeners also share his curiosity.

I am asked "How do vultures manage to locate a carcass on the ground from a height at which they themselves appear like microscopic midges in the sky. Is it by sight or by smell?"

Of the senses possessed by birds, eyesight and hearing seem to be the highest developed. Taste and smell are almost wanting. Birds that subsist on animal food – those for instance that capture flies and beetles in the air, and the birds of prey like hawks and eagles, possess extraordinarily well-developed eyesight. A fly-catcher will dart at a midge fully twenty-five yards away and quite invisible to the human eye, and snap it up in mid-air. A blackbird will detect an earthworm wriggling on a lawn at over

*4 February 1951, Bombay.

a hundred feet distance. In addition to keenness of sight a bird's eyes have the power of altering their focus instantaneously – in effect to change from a telescope to a microscope in a fraction of time. For fast-flying birds which capture minute winged insects in the air, like the flycatchers, or which hurl themselves at other birds with lightning speed, like the falcons, it is easy to understand that this power of rapid accommodation of the eye is of the greatest advantage. Although vultures belong to the same tribe as the birds of prey, their food, unlike that of the falcons and some eagles, consists mainly of carrion and has not to be hunted down when alive. Their eyesight is certainly very keen, but the keenness has been somewhat overestimated. At any time of the day, numbers of vultures may be seen in the sky, sailing majestically on motionless outspread wings, quartering large sections of the countryside. The birds are all flying at different levels, some maybe at only 200 ft, others at 4000 ft, a height that is said to yield the optimum breadth of view. Now it is not reasonable to suppose that the highest bird would be capable of spotting a dead bullock on the ground so far below it, and often partly hidden from view. What actually happens is that the higher-flying birds are keeping a sharp lookout, not so much for carcasses directly as for the slightest sign from their low-flying brethren that food has been sighted. The bird closest to the ground is usually the first to discover a carcass and descends to it. The one above him perceives the move and promptly follows suit, and so on and on till the last vulture drops out of the limitless blue to join the ghoulish feast. This process has been graphically described in the memorable lines of Hiawatha. Says the poet –

> Never stoops the soaring vulture
> On his quarry in the desert,
> On the sick or wounded bison,
> But another vulture watching from his high aerial lookout

Sees the downward plunge and follows.
And a third pursues the second, coming from the invisible ether
First a speck and then a vulture
Till the air is dark with pinions.

Repeated experiments to test the smelling powers of birds have shown that this sense is non-existent, or at most very poorly developed. Partially decomposed, strong-smelling meat hidden under the end of a ground sheet in a vulture's cage, upon which the hungry bird was actually walking about, failed to produce any response from it. But as soon as the meat was uncovered and exposed to view, the vulture fell upon it greedily. Similar experiments with other species of birds have consistently produced the same negative results. Nevertheless, some hunters of experience maintain that certain duck species do possess keen smelling powers.

To sportsmen who go after tiger and panther it is well known that to protect a "kill" of one of these large cats from the attentions of vultures during daytime, it is only necessary to cover up the carcass with leaves and branches so that the birds do not see it from the air. If the carcass is properly covered it will be safe, no matter how much to the high heavens it may smell! That vultures occasionally do discover such carcasses notwithstanding is due not to their "following their noses", as is sometimes alleged, but to clues furnished them by jackals prowling around the carcass and the crows that have gathered on their heels.

While on the subject of eyesight, it is interesting that experiments, though they are not always easy to interpret, suggest that, unlike mammals which are believed to be colour blind, seeing objects only as in a black and white photographic print, birds possess marked colour perception. But they apparently cannot see blues and violets at all. It is pointed out that if we wore reddish-yellow glasses our colour perception would be like a bird's. Red seems to be the colour most attractive to birds. Thus the majority of what are known as "bird-flowers" – meaning the flowers that depend for their fertilisation more or less entirely upon the activities of nectar-eating birds – are nearly always some shade of crimson or scarlet to attract their visitors.

Another question which one faces quite frequently from listeners is how migratory birds, often without experience or guidance, find their way to distant corners of the earth over thousands of miles of featureless land and sea.

It must be admitted that in spite of the great amount of factual data on bird migration that has been accumulated in recent years through worldwide international collaboration, especially through the method of banding or ringing migratory birds, much of the *How* and *Why* remains as great a mystery as before. It seems unlikely that satisfactory answers will ever be found, but experiments and conjecture are continuing.

One novel speculation that enjoyed popularity and varying degrees of acceptance, until experiments more or less conclusively exploded it, was that birds were in some particular way sensitive to terrestrial magnetism and were guided to their goal by this force. Magnets attached to the bodies of migrating birds, and other devices to counteract the earth's magnetism, however, failed to deflect the birds from their traditional course, and the hypothesis has since lost much of its popular appeal. Perhaps the most promising line of investigation today is the one recently started by a German scientist and reported at the International Ornithological Congress in Sweden in 1950. Dr Gustav Kramer found that during the migration period starlings kept in a suitable cage would perch or flutter towards the direction in which they would have flown had they been free. By a clever arrangement of mirrors he proved that it is the direction of the sun's light that determines the direction chosen by migrating or would-be migrating birds. By manipulating mirrors at a number of openings round the cage he could induce the birds which normally gathered towards the south-west to gather at the opposite or north-east end, or halfway round towards north-west. Here at last we have some more tangible basis to build upon than the purely speculative "innate sense of direction" or the hypothetical reliance on the earth's magnetism. Dr Kramer's work is being followed with great interest by students of bird migration throughout the world.

Talking of bird migration, people are interested to learn where most of our common winter migrants come from, where they go, and how precise information concerning them is collected.

Observations made more or less continuously over the last seventy years and more by competent bird students – chiefly British civil and military officials posted along our north-western frontier – have furnished much of the overall knowledge that we now possess concerning the migratory movements of birds in India, chiefly wild duck and other sporting birds. The purely observational method has its limitations, however; for instance it cannot tell us precisely where an individual bird comes from in autumn, or its destination when it departs in spring. The only reliable way of ascertaining these and many other facts concerning the life histories of individual birds is by marking them. This is the modern method of migration study, and it is practised on a worldwide scale. It consists of fastening a light aluminium ring on the leg of a bird that has been trapped or netted or taken young in the nest. The ring bears a number and the address of a registered ringing station. According to international agreement, private individuals' addresses are discouraged as far as possible, and only rings issued by recognised institutions are used. In India our rings bear the name of the Bombay Natural History Society. Particulars of the ringed bird are kept in a special register so that if it is ever killed or otherwise reported, its case history can be readily traced. When a sufficient number of such recoveries have been obtained, it is possible to extract a great deal of varied information from them.

Compared with the gigantic scale upon which ringing work is done in the U.S. and many European countries, our efforts in India have been negligible. They have, nevertheless, provided us with practically all the authentic data we possess. The recoveries of Indian ringed ducks in the U.S.S.R., and of Russian ringed birds in India have nicely complemented each other to provide first-hand information of where our ducks come from and where they go. Mallards ringed in Bahawalpur and Sind for instance, were recovered in Russia at distances upward of 2300 miles, and data concerning the breeding grounds and winter quarters of many other species of wildfowl have also been similarly obtained. Two of the longest migratory journeys were made by a Pintail and a Redcrested Pochard, respectively. The former ringed in Dhar (Central India), now Madhya Bharat, was recovered in Siberia at a distance of 2800 miles. The latter, ringed in Sind, was killed on Lake Baikal, also in Siberia, about 2700 miles away. The round trip made by these birds to and from their breeding grounds must therefore be well over 5500 miles – no mean annual performance even for such a strong-flying bird as a wild duck.

6

Interview with Dr Bernhard Rensch, Director of the Zoological Department, University of Munster, West Germany*

Q-1: We have in the Studios Dr Bernhard Rensch, who is Director of the Zoological Department of the University of Münster in West Germany. Dr Rensch is the leader of a zoological expedition to India. But perhaps I am anticipating him. Professor Rensch, do tell us about the object of your visit and the scope of your studies.

Dr R: Well, it is not so easy to answer this question sufficiently. Of course we have our scientific programme comprehending many different problems of our special fields of zoological and physiological research, problems which are to be solved only in India and which we began to work out already in our Zoological Department of the Münster-University in Western Germany during the last few years. But the motive of our coming arises also from deeper roots. During my whole life I have looked to India with ardent desire. This marvellous country with its interesting animals and plants is not only a paradise for every biologist, it is not only full of wonderful old temples, buildings, and sculptures

*15 March 1953, Bombay (assumed).

of aesthetic perfection, it is also a country of highly fascinating religions and of philosophical systems, which have already allured so many Germans and which were already admired by Goethe, by Schopenhauer, by Deussen, by Max Müller, and by so many others. And at last India is a country of highly interesting men. And the first of them, with whom I became acquainted twenty-four years ago, my old friend Sálim Ali, the leading ornithologist of this country, knew very well how to raise my enthusiasm. And when we last met in my home at Münster, two years ago, I had to promise him to come out to India one day. Well, that day was now the 28th of February, when a large English boat set us ashore in Bombay.

But now you want to hear a little more in detail, what we want to do in India. At first we have the intention to study animal behaviour and parallel with this we want to collect and preserve the brains of some animals for future anatomical and microscopical research, when we are back in Germany. For, the general problem which we have tackled in Germany concerns the connection between the microscopical structure of brains and the behaviour, that is to say the special instincts and the special capabilities of learning. We know relatively little about this connection, although many investigations were conducted during the last fifty years. One of the special questions connected with this general problem is the question, whether a larger brain is capable to develop more complicated instincts, to learn more or more complicated things, or to retain for a longer time. Therefore, we have to compare the brains of nearly related larger and smaller animals. In Germany we only have very small squirrels, small bats, and shrews, but here in India there are also large species of these kinds. There are the large flying foxes, there are giant squirrels and large shrews, the so-called musk-rats. All these brains will serve as models for inquiries about questions, which are also of interest with respect to the functioning of the human brain.

Q-2: Is there any animal in India in which you are specially interested?

Dr R: Yes. One of the most interesting animals with regard to brain size is the elephant, having the largest brain of all land mammals, the animal which had to give his head for Ganesha, the godhead of wisdom *must* be a very intelligent being. Therefore already in Germany we tried to find out something about his intelligence. Of course we had to do this in an exact scientific manner. Our young elephant, in the zoo at Münster, was trained to distinguish a series of different patterns. He had to learn the difference between a cross and a triangle, between broad and small stripes, between three black points and four black points, and so on. At last our elephant mastered twelve different tasks at the same time by choosing always the right pattern and by avoiding the wrong one. And after three months without any training the elephant still knew all the tasks very well and made nearly no mistakes. Such a long period of retaining a large number of different patterns seems to be a rare exception among mammals. Thus, now we are anxious to teach ourselves a little more about the elephant's intelligence. We want to watch working elephants, to see how many human words they comprehend and whether they show some real insight in the sense of human reasoning when they meet with difficult situations. We also want to make a little film of working elephants for scientific purposes. Perhaps this can be done in Mysore.

Q-3: I suppose climate of a country has a bearing on the problems that you are going to study.

Dr R: Yes. In India we want specially to know how a tropical climate acts upon an animal. To elucidate this we intend to compare geographical races of these Indian animals, which are represented in Europe, too. For instance the house sparrow, the skylark, the oriole, the grey titmice, and other birds are the same in both regions, but the Indian races are always smaller, they have relatively longer feet and bills, they lay fewer eggs, and so on. Now, we also want to know whether the interior organs are also different. Therefore we have to weigh and to measure these organs of the mentioned species and compare them with the weights and the measurements of the German races. I also want to count the number of blood cells and so on. In such a way we hope to understand a little more about the alteration of a species under the influence of a tropical climate.

Q-4: And now will you tell us about the composition of your team?

Dr R: I am accompanied by my three assistants, by Dr Miss Nolte, by Dr Harde, and Dr Altevogt, and by my wife who is also working scientifically. Each of us is a specialist in certain scientific fields. Dr Harde is a specialist for the microscopical research of the brains of mammals, Dr Miss Nolte for the brains of amphibians and reptiles, Dr Altevogt for animal behaviour, and my wife for the anatomy of other organs. But we do not only work as a team. Besides, each of us has also his special problems. Dr Altevogt wants to study the nocturnal lizards, having the capability to adhere on polished glass or even walk upside down on a ceiling. How they can perform this is still known very imperfectly. Dr Harde, Dr Nolte, and my wife are also interested in the relations between the habitat of an animal and its anatomical structure and other questions.

At last we are also anxious to see the biological institutions in India. We are kindly invited to participate in a scientific congress in Delhi concerning organic evolution. Furthermore we intend to deliver some lectures in Indian universities, and I already did so in the famous old Bombay Natural History Society. In this way we hope to come in closer contact with our Indian colleagues, and moreover we hope that this connection may be strengthened in future times. Our university at Münster in Western Germany, which was totally destroyed during the war, is rebuilt now to a rather large extent. Especially our institutions of Natural Sciences are now rather comfortable and well equipped with the most modern scientific instruments of every kind. We would have great pleasure to have here also Indian students in future, and I may assure that we will welcome there also every Indian colleague very heartily.

7

Trends in Modern Bird Study*

THANKS TO THE great diversity in its physical features, climate, and vegetation, India is particularly rich in bird life. The six volumes on birds of that remarkable semi-official series, the *Fauna of British India*, covered the entire so-called British Indian Empire, including undivided India, Burma, and Ceylon, and described some 2300 species and geographical races of birds. Nearly 500 of these are winter visitors from countries beyond our northern frontiers. With the removal of Burma and Ceylon, a number of forms peculiar to those rather different physiographical areas can now be expunged. The separation of Pakistan makes little material difference to the residuary Indian total, since, happily, birds are not civilised enough to recognise barriers of politics or religion!

Some portions of the Indian subcontinent are amongst the richest areas in the world as regards species and numbers of birds. Sikkim, for instance, with an area of less than 3000 sq. miles can boast of over 550 forms.

Almost all the scientific data we possess on Indian birds are due to the voluntary exertions of a successive band of enthusiastic

*20 September 1955, Bombay.

amateur naturalists, almost entirely foreigners, chiefly British officers of the armed and civil services. Of these A.O. Hume (incidentally one of the founders of the Indian National Congress) was perhaps the most outstanding. They collected bird specimens diligently in whatever corner of India they happened to be stationed. The accumulated results of their activities are now to be seen in the British Museum in London, which today possesses perhaps the most complete collection of Indian birds in the world. More methodical fieldwork, though less extensive collecting, has been done within the last three decades, mostly by Indian workers, and many of the gaps in the knowledge of the distribution of Indian birds have been filled. We have thus reached a stage where further desultory collecting, on the off chance of discovering a new species, is unnecessary. There are, however, a few areas still left which are insufficiently explored, and a few groups of birds and individual species requiring closer morphological study. But these are subjects which can profitably be tackled only by the competent student with a proper scientific background and an understanding of the problems involved.

Most of the activities of workers so far have centred on the collecting of skins, and on their naming and classification, and also on collecting of nests and eggs. Unfortunately the most vital and dynamic part of bird study – the study of the live bird – was badly neglected. The result is that while we know by name and description all the birds that are found in the country, our knowledge of almost every aspect of their life histories is almost nil. In most European countries and in the U.S.A., where the hobby so-called bird watching is much more popular and widespread, very substantial progress has been achieved in the field study of living birds, and meticulous investigations on the food, behaviour, social habits, population dynamics, courtship, song, migration, and ecology have brought to light a large amount of unsuspected and often astounding facts leading to the better understanding of the bird's place in the scheme of nature. Significant advances are being continually made in every department of bird study by means of well-planned and ingenious experimentation in the laboratory, and persevering co-operative studies in the field. Particularly valuable work is being done by the Edward Grey Institute of Field Ornithology, which is now recognised by the University of Oxford as a school for postgraduate ornithological field research. There is a mistaken tendency among persons who take to the study of birds in our country to imagine that once they have acquired a certain degree of proficiency, with the help of a coloured picture book, in identifying a bird – for instance telling a parakeet from, say, a bee-eater – they have learnt all there is to know about birds, and that further pursuit of the subject would be unprofitable, unless they made a collection of skins. Yet it is just at this point that real bird study must begin. Recognising birds in the field with tolerable accuracy is in essence like learning the alphabet. It is the essential minimum qualification for the proper intellectual and aesthetic enjoyment of birds, and for making useful contributions to scientific knowledge. It is no longer necessary to collect further stacks of mouldy skins in order to do so.

Perhaps there is no better index of the diverse channels into which modern bird study is striking out, and the expanse of the field it covers, than the titles of papers read at the two post-war International Ornithological Congresses, the first held at Uppsala, Sweden, in 1950, and the second at Basel, Switzerland, in 1954, at both of which India was unofficially represented.

I would say that the present trends in the scientific study of birds lie in three main directions, besides of course Evolution and Systematics. This last is being tackled both from the field and the laboratory angle, involving morphology, cytology, genetics, and biometry, and often leading to seeming abstractions which would appear to the layman to have no connection whatsoever with birds!

By and large, however, the accent today is all on field work, and Ecology, Population Dynamics, and Behaviour dominate the scene.

Ecology, for those unfamiliar with the word, is the part of biology that deals with the relationship of an organism to its environment. The fact that some species of animals thrive under given natural conditions, whereas superficially closely related forms cannot do so, is based upon the interaction of a whole host of ecological factors not understood until carefully investigated. A great deal of very thorough ecological work is being conducted on many individual species and populations of birds, and results of the most remarkable and unsuspected kind are being brought to light. There is such an intricate ramification of these factors that no measures for the protection of birds, for instance, can succeed without a careful consideration of the complete ecology of the species in question.

Ecological studies of birds, particularly in regard to their population dynamics or cyclic fluctuation in numbers, and their food and feeding habits, have a definite bearing on human economics, more directly in the spheres of agriculture and forestry. It is unfortunate that in India the economic importance of bird life is not sufficiently recognised or appreciated. This lack of appreciation, I feel, is one of our main stumbling blocks and perhaps the chief reason why the majority of zoology students at our Indian universities turn to the study of insects and fishes to the complete neglect of ornithology. Indirectly this is also why zoology teachers encourage their students to do so, since there is a prospect, however hazy, of getting a job as an entomologist or a fisheries officer in the appropriate government department, whereas ornithology dangles not even the ghost of such a prospect.

Economic considerations alone dictate that proper life-history studies of Indian birds should be undertaken on the model and along the lines of the admirable techniques developed in many European countries, the U.S.S.R., and in the U.S.A. Economic ornithology is so closely bound up with Economic Entomology and Economic Botany that it seems illogical for it to be so badly neglected when the other two have so amply justified themselves.

I emphasise the economic aspect of bird study because I believe that not until ornithology can offer some prospect of a livelihood to its would-be devotees will it be possible, in a poor country like ours, to produce the required personnel to follow the modern scientific methods of bird study and to evolve new and profitable trends with the rich material and especial natural advantages at our disposal, and to line up with the advances being made in countries less favoured by Nature.

Some very remarkable lines of investigation are being pursued in the study of the theoretical aspects of bird migration. One of the principal mysteries connected with the problem of migration, as we know, is as to the manner in which birds navigate or orientate themselves. How some young birds, for instance, without previous experience or learning, find their way over hundreds of miles of land and sea to a prescribed goal, fixed through generations, but of which they can have no knowledge: in other words to their exact winter quarters in autumn, and back to their ancestral home, or breeding ground, in spring. Many theories have been put forward from time to time to explain this mystery. Though all of them found protagonists for a time, they had to be discarded one by one, as more critical study became possible. Ingenious experiments by a German scientist in post-war years have shown fairly convincingly that direction-finding or navigation – either innate, as in the young bird on its first migratory journey, or in an older bird with the added experience of previous journeys, is based on the sun – the angle it makes with the earth at the appropriate seasons and at certain times of the day. Having taken the primary direction from the sun (possibly polarised light), the bird is able to maintain a steady course, up to a point, even on a cloudy day or while flying at night. It is of course too early as yet to be dogmatic; but it does look as if at last we are on something like the right track. Experiments are continuing both under natural and controlled conditions, and the results hold great promise. Birds are known to have a very accurate perception of chronometer time and an inborn sense of the general migration trends in spring and autumn.

While this suggests a way in which birds may navigate over a course with no visible landmarks to guide them, it does not at all answer the question how inexperienced birds determine the goal to be made for, and how they realise the fact when they have arrived there. Indeed some of the mysteries connected with the migration of birds seem hardly likely ever to be solved. A vast amount of factual basic data concerning migration are being accumulated through the method of ringing, or banding, migratory birds, which is being practised on a very large scale in Russia and many European countries, and also in the U.S.A.

A somewhat sensational offshoot of ornithology has proved to be the study of the parasitic mallophaga or feather-lice of birds. Mallophaga are host-specific to such a degree that one species of the parasites cannot live if transferred to a bird-host of a different family, or in some cases of a different genus, or even species. A close study of mallophaga in recent years has suggested their possibilities as indicators as having great significance in the study of Evolution. To give an example, for a long time there was controversy over the true systematic position of the flamingo. On various anatomical considerations some authorities were inclined to place it with the storks and herons, while other maintained that it possessed closer affinity with the ducks and geese. A study of the mallopaga inhabiting the flamingo showed that the species were identical or closely allied to those found in the duck family, but were totally unrelated to any found on storks and herons. This strong supporting evidence helped to settle the issue, and it is now generally conceded that the flamingo is merely a modified first cousin of the goose.

8

Talking as an Ornithologist*

ONE OF THE STANDARD questions that I, as an ornithologist, inevitably have to face is about what thrilling adventures I have had in a lifetime of exploring for birds. I fear that my standard answer to this must seem disappointing to those who expect to hear tales of derring-do. Ornithology as a hobby, or profession or persuasion – whatever one may choose to call it – though full of adventures and rewards and disappointments, is by its very nature one of the most peaceable pursuits of the out-of-doors. It is certainly not lacking in excitements and thrills, though these may be of a different kind from what the average enquirer imagines. The excitement lies in ferreting out clues and then following them up step by step to the discovery or confirmation of a fact or facts or to the refutation of unwarranted beliefs, about which one has formed a hunch. Thus one of the most satisfying and rewarding thrills was when, in the earlier days of my bird watching, some thirty-five years ago I hit upon, rather accidentally than by design, the first rational interpretation of the peculiar breeding biology of our common weaver bird, the Baya. I had been brought up only on the traditional accounts of its nesting habits as recorded in the literature

*25 March 1969, Delhi.

which had come down from book to book. These accounts were interesting enough in themselves for a keen bird photographer to want to record them on film. But while concealed in a canvas hide perched on top of a 10 ft step-ladder and within a few feet of the nests, I noticed some unorthodox goings on in the colony which clearly suggested that the birds had not read my textbooks! A few hours in this hide each day, and copious notes and diagrams of the proceedings in the colony soon gave me a pretty good idea of what was actually happening, till at the end of a few weeks it was even possible to speculate with some confidence on the general pattern of the Baya's breeding biology. Since then the new interpretation has had plenty of opportunity for being tested and retested and confirmed by myself and other bird students, and, with additional refinements, is now accepted as what might be called the "Authorised Version". In brief, the findings were as follows: the male Baya, who in his breeding livery is a handsome little sparrow-like bird – largely brilliant golden yellow – is an artful polygamist. He may acquire any number of wives from two to four – sometimes even five – not all in a flock in harem style, but one by one progressively, depending upon his capacity to provide them each with a suitable home. The male alone is responsible for building the nest; the female has no hand in it. Males normally select a babool or palm tree to hang their compactly woven retort-shaped structures, and several males build together in a colony which may sometimes contain a hundred nests or more. At a particular stage in the architecture, when the nest is about half-finished, there comes suddenly one fine morning an invasion by a party of female Bayas, all eagerly prospecting for desirable homes. They arrive at the colony amidst great noise and excitement from the welcoming males, and calmly and deliberately visit nest after nest – to assess its workmanship as it were. Some nests are approved, others are rejected. While the examination is in progress the builder clings on the outside of the nest, excitedly flapping his wings in obvious invitation and while awaiting her pleasure and verdict. If a female is satisfied with the structure she just takes possession of it and by that very fact becomes the builder's wife. Thereafter the cock works feverishly to complete the nest with its long entrance tube. The female lays her eggs within, incubates them, and brings up the family. This is entirely her department, and it is seldom that the cock helps her at all in foraging for the chicks. Having settled wife No. 1 in the nest, the male immediately proceeds to commence a second one a few feet away. At the appropriate stage, another female in search of a suitable home may, in like manner, take possession of this nest, and the whole process is then repeated once again. Thus the male may find himself the happy husband of several wives and the proud father of several families at practically one and the same time! It happens not infrequently that for some reason female after female fails to approve a particular nest. Undeterred, the male abandons this built structure and promptly commences to try again. In every Baya colony are always to be found a number of such half-built and abandoned nests. This is the real explanation for them; unfortunately not the more poetic and popular one, that these so-called "cock nests" are specially built by the male to swing himself as he sings love songs to beguile the tedium of his incubating spouse nearby!

With the richness and variety of the bird life in India, exciting discoveries of a similar kind are waiting to be made by every birdwatcher who has the necessary enthusiasm and patience and perseverance. As yet the devotees of this hobby are few and far between, but it is refreshing to find that bird watching is rapidly growing in popularity along with other civilised cultural outdoor pursuits.

While the field study of birds is a peaceful enough occupation, it is not entirely without occasional physical thrills and even hazards. In elephant-ridden jungles in South India, for instance, one can frequently find oneself in highly disturbing and uncomfortable situations. A wild elephant suddenly come upon at close quarters – by no means an uncommon occurrence in part of Mysore and Kerala – can be an unnerving experience, almost invariably resulting in the undignified spectacle (for the elephant) of the ornithologist in full flight in the opposite direction! In actual fact there is little danger of a deliberate attack by an elephant unless it happens to be a rogue or a female accompanied by a small calf. However, it is bad diplomacy in close-up situations to wait for this to become apparent before taking the only reasonable course. For it may well be that in tall-grass country even the most well-meaning stampede by a frightened herd may result in the ornithologist turning an unwitting casualty. Therefore discretion and not valour is what such situations obviously demand.

9

The Usefulness of Birds to Animals and Man*

As nature conservationists we are often asked why, in spite of the enormous damage birds so obviously do to food crops and in other ways, we still persist in our lunatic advocacy for the protection and preservation of these destructive pests. This doubt of our sanity may to some extent seem excusable in the simple cultivator whose sole contact with birds is through the damage he suffers from them as he helplessly watches the hungry hordes descending upon his ripening fields day after day to rob him of the lawful fruits of his months of toil and sweat. And even the most ardent conservationist will admit that locally some birds can be destructive to agriculture in the highest degree and may call for drastic measures of control. Perhaps small wonder then that those who suffer from their depredations should single-mindedly pray for some magic mantra that will rid them of this constant menace for all time. Indeed I have heard politicians sonorously declaim that in the interest of the poor downtrodden cultivator all birds and other wild animals that damage his crops or cattle should be completely wiped out. Yet, the problem is far less simple than he thinks. Short cuts of the drastic kind suggested

*29 July 1967, Bombay.

by our politician friend may not only prove longer in the long run but are certain to raise greater problems by upsetting the balance of nature in a way that may even make agriculture itself, and all other forms of human activity, impossible. The main trouble is that while the harmfulness of birds – for example their ravages to ripening cereal crops – is plain for all to see and condemn, their usefulness is exerted in more subtle and indirect ways and is not so blatantly advertised. Take the case of the sparrows and weaver birds which, at face value, are certainly amongst the most destructive bird pests of crops in the country as a whole. The damage caused to cereals by members of this prolific family has been variously estimated at between 15 and 40 per cent of the total crop, depending upon local conditions. Although rather rough and ready, and seldom based on strictly scientific data, the estimates are clearly indicative of the seriousness of the damage, which cannot be cheerfully condoned. What possible claim can such birds have to consideration from the farmer whose labours and hopes they have so cruelly blasted? The claim is this. The staple food of adult sparrows and weaver birds is grain. During the greater part of the year, when there are no crops to raid, they subsist quite respectably on grass- and weed seeds, and by gleaning such grain as has been left scattered about in the harvested fields. At that time also they do some very useful service by eating a quantum of moths and other insects, most of them harmful to crops. During the season of cultivation, chiefly the monsoon, much of the food is obtained by raiding standing crops, but at the same time the birds also devour large quantities of insects in the self-same fields. It happens that the breeding season of most seed-eating birds synchronises with the season of *kharif* crops, which is also the heyday for the multiplication of insect pests. While adult weaver birds and sparrows live largely on seeds and grain, their nestlings, from the time they hatch out up till flying from the nest, require soft-bodied insect food – more or less exclusively at first. The majority of these insects are serious agricultural pests and under favourable weather conditions their numbers are often liable to irrupt in plague proportions. Thus at one and the same time the birds are performing the double role of protectors and destroyers of the crops. The total population of sparrows and weaver birds in India must, on a modest estimate, run into hundreds of millions. They produce on an average two or three young per nest, which are fed during the entire nestling period of about two weeks almost exclusively on caterpillars and grubs and soft-bodied insects. When it is recalled that young birds in the first few days of their lives consume more than their own weight of food in twenty-four hours, some idea can be obtained of the enormous good these birds must silently do during the nestling period to counterbalance the damage so loudly proclaimed. And these birds are just two groups out of the hundreds of species that are helping in this way to preserve the balance of nature, of which man himself is the immediate beneficiary.

The owls have been bracketed with the diurnal birds of prey – both equally unjustly – as enemies of game birds and domestic poultry, and are often destroyed out of hand. The smaller owls live chiefly on mice and insects, of which the prolific locust and grasshopper form a considerable proportion. They must therefore be ranked as wholly beneficial to man. Some of the larger owls will occasionally take game birds and poultry if readily available, but the staple diet of most species is rats and mice, some of the most destructive pests that man and his works suffer from. Rats are as notoriously voracious as they are fecund. Many species breed throughout the year, starting when only about 14 weeks old, and are capable of producing 6 litters of an average 8 young each, per year. Arithmetic will show that at this rate – assuming that the sexes are equal and there are no deaths – a single pair would increase in five years to well over 940 billion rats (I hope billion is the right word – my answer runs into twelve digits!). This is of course a purely theoretical computation, and nature would never allow such an enormity to be achieved, but it just shows the colossal potentiality for increase possessed by this pestilential family. A study of the food of some of the larger owls shows that two rats a piece per night is perhaps an underestimate of the food eaten by them. According to our rat-multiplication formula, as above, it can be worked out that every pair of rats destroyed by an owl means the annual suppression of a potential increase of 880 rats! When it is remembered that the owls are engaged in the good work night after night, and from year's end to year's end, some idea of the untold good they silently do can be obtained.

In India today, where the emphasis rightly is on growing more food, it seems anomalous that the focus should all be on the damage that birds do to crops and their beneficent activities should be so completely and consistently ignored. There are no voices raised in defence of birds save for a few forlorn ones in the wilderness, which do not seem to matter. It is true that, like most other blessings, birds are also not an unmixed one. But what is urgently needed at this juncture, side by side with every other effort to produce more food, is a proper scientific assessment of the true status of the various bird species implicated in the agricultural and economic welfare of the country. Since the roles of adult birds and young can be so contradictory, it is essential that the investigations should cover the entire life history of the bird, including its food and feeding habits in all seasons, in population structure and dynamics. In this way alone will it be possible to strike an accurate balance sheet, as it were, of the credit and debit sides of each species to serve as a reliable basis for any measures that may later be deemed necessary, either to encourage or control its abundance.

But I realise that in spite of the title I have so far said nothing about the usefulness of birds to animals as distinct from man. As far as man's livestock is concerned the impact of wild birds on domestic animals is, directly or indirectly, little different from that on man, the interests of the two having become largely compatible. Between wild animals and birds a wide range of symbiotic relationships exist from which, as a rule, both parties to the transaction reap substantial benefits. A familiar example of this sort of relationship may be seen in wild buffaloes and the cattle egret. While seeking its food the bird renders useful service to its partners by ridding them of tiresome parasites such as ticks and leeches. Examples of this kind can be multiplied, and in some cases shown to possess far more vital connections. But the chiefest usefulness of birds to other animals is perhaps as the important links they constitute in the food chains, both in the role of predator and predated, and in thus helping to maintain the delicate balance which the constant meddling by man with Nature could easily upset.

10

The Role of Birds in Agriculture and Forestry*

THE SUFFERING CULTIVATOR may find it hard to detect a method in the madness, as he believes, of those who clamour for the protection and conservation of birds. Birds plunder his crops in broad daylight; their criminal mischief and ravages are plain for all to see and are sufficiently self-condemning. Why then should any consideration be shown to these destructive pests? Surely their complete removal from the scene would ensure richer harvests and more food for the hungry millions. So argues the suffering cultivator, and so feel the well-meaning people who would ameliorate his woes overnight.

Against these there are others, equally well-meaning but perhaps better informed, who believe that without the constant and unrelenting check exercised on insect pests by birds, no vegetation could exist on Earth, and without vegetation life itself would be impossible. It may not be easy to convince the aggrieved cultivator of this argument when his hard-won crops have just been so badly ravished by birds that it is perhaps not even worth his while to salvage what is left. Yet, in the long-term view, there

*9 July 1973, Bombay.

is much substance in the conservationist's reasoning, as I shall presently try to show.

The variety, fecundity, and voracity of insects are colossal. Over 30,000 species of insects have been described from the Indian subcontinent alone. This is more than twenty-five times the total species of birds. Many of the insects are destructive pests of food crops, economic timbers, and other forest produce: many are harmful to livestock directly or indirectly, and many are vectors of diseases often fatal to man himself. The fecundity of insects is phenomenal: a single pair of the American Colorado Beetle, which belongs to a family of notorious crop pests in India, is estimated to increase to 60 million individuals in a single season if allowed unchecked multiplication. Thanks to natural checks, however, this figure is never likely to be attained in practice; nevertheless it is a measure of the proven reproductive power of insects. As to voracity, insects – especially in their early stages as caterpillars or grubs – have astounding appetites. Some caterpillars will eat twice their own weight in green leaves in a day. Locusts have been a dreaded scourge throughout Man's history. Their migratory swarms are sometimes so thick as to obscure the sun, and such a visitation can reduce all crops and greenery over hundreds of square kilometres to a desert of bare stalks in the matter of a few hours. It is obvious that with such astounding rates of reproduction and feeding potential, it would not take long for all vegetation on Earth to disappear unless the hungry hordes were kept under rigid and relentless control. In maintaining such control, birds are one of the most important natural forces working in close collaboration with predaceous and parasitic insects.

Birds themselves also have prodigious appetites. The rate of their metabolism is higher than mammals, and the energy demands for swift aerial locomotion renders feedings in birds a continuous process. By the same token, therefore, birds have been traditionally stigmatised as the cultivator's foes. It is true that in some localities and in certain situations the damage caused by birds to cereal crops may be quite appalling. But there are few species whose harmfulness to agriculture and horticulture is so clear-cut and unequivocal as the green parakeets, especially our common Rose-ringed species. At no stage of their life cycle do the parakeets eat insects: they live and batten entirely on grain and fruit chiefly marauded in fields and orchards. They have wasteful feeding habits and destroy far more than they actually consume. The dense swarms in which parakeets commit their depredations on crops makes them a very serious pest, and they need drastic control without compunction. Not so, however, the several other birds – for example the weavers and related members of the sparrow family – which seem to suffer universal condemnation. While equally destructive, seemingly, they nevertheless play a distinctly double-sided role. Under natural conditions these birds subsist mainly on grass-seeds. They live in moderate-sized flocks which move about the countryside in quest of food. Their populations are then regulated and kept in reasonable bounds by the limited food supply and natural predators. But Man has upset the balance by the monoculture of cereals over extensive areas, thereby creating an unnatural excess of food for these birds, as well as for insects. Taking advantage of this superabundance, weaver birds and sparrows band themselves into vast flocks of many thousand strong and undoubtedly cause enormous damage to ripening crops. Even so their true economic status in cultivated areas is hard to assess. It is an intricate complex of debits and credits, varying from downright harmful to predominantly beneficial. In other words they are the cultivator's foes in some situations and his allies in others. For it must be remembered that although the sparrow tribe subsists largely on grain as adults, their nestlings in early life, and they themselves while nesting, feed largely if not entirely on caterpillars and soft-bodied insects. Many of these are destructive agricultural pests, and possibly taken in the very fields where the direct ravages of the birds were committed.

Owls and hawks, though largely persecuted through ignorant superstition or for alleged misdemeanours, are beneficial in the highest degree in keeping down the population of rats and mice, and suchlike vermin. These rodents, as is only too well known, are amongst our most destructive non-insect pests of agriculture and forestry. The overall loss of foodgrains in the country attributed to rats and mice is well over 10 per cent of the entire production, and in some localities their depredations are truly staggering. Like insects, rats and mice are also astoundingly fecund. It has been reliably computed that a single pair of rats, given equal sexes and no deaths, would increase to 880 rats at the end of the year. This figure is hypothetical and happily never likely to be attained in nature; but it is not an extravagant pointer to the breeding potential of these rodents. Many of our owls subsist predominantly on rodents; from examination of their stomach contents it seems more than probable that a single owl takes two to three or more rats or mice in the course of a night's hunting. Even the destruction of just two rats per night would mean the suppression of a potential annual increase of 880 rats. And when it is realised that the birds are engaged in the good work for 365 nights, year after year, the magnitude of their beneficent service to agriculture and forestry can be appreciated in correct perspective.

Bird study from the economic point of view has not yet received due recognition in India. The unwisdom of taking drastic short-cuts to control bird (or other animal) populations, without a proper scientific understanding of their ecology, has been demonstrated again and again in many countries. The recent excessive zeal to exterminate the sparrow in China under the loudly drummed "Cultural Revolution" programme is a case in point.

The campaign apparently boomeranged in the shape of redoubled onslaughts by insect hordes freed from the effective control of birds, and the operation had to be abandoned. For a scientific and meaningful assessment of the double-edged impact of birds on human affairs – for striking a proper balance sheet of their debits and credits, as it were – accurate knowledge of their complete life histories is essential. We need to know their ecology – their food and feeding habits in all seasons and at all ages, their biomass and their population dynamics. In a country like India, so vitally dependent on agriculture and forests, research on the economic status of birds should have received high priority in agricultural strategy long ago but it did not. However, the recent Symposium on Economic Ornithology, held in Bombay under the joint auspices of the Indian Council of Agricultural Research and the Bombay Natural History Society, was a useful and encouraging exercise, and also a happy token of assurance that the Powers That Be are at last alive to the importance of this research. If it leads to the establishment of calls for research in Economic Ornithology, at least in all our Agricultural Universities, it will mean a significant step forward in our efforts to Grow More Food.

Adequate, wisely maintained forests, apart from their direct economic benefits, constitute Nature's strongest insurance against floods and drought such as we have been experiencing of late. The role of birds in the maintenance of healthy stands of trees has been amply appreciated in the more developed countries, and also that any damage they may sometimes do is only local and transitory. The beneficial impact of birds on forests has been more clearly demonstrated since the practice of the commercial management of forests to produce a single species of tree has become more general. Fewer birds in such forests, owing to absence of tree-holes and shrubbery for nesting and feeding, means greater risks from plant diseases. A well-formed tree, such as managed forests aim to produce, is unsuitable for a hole-nesting bird. Therefore when clear-felling natural forests to replant with commercial species such as conifers, it is the practice in modern forestry to diversify the habitat by retaining a few overmature stems and "islands" of broad-leaved coppices as temporary shelters for the new crop as well as feeding and nesting sites for birds. Provision of nest-boxes and "shelves" offers additional inducement to birds. This practice deserves to be adopted in India in cases of monoculture of exotic species such as Eucalyptus, pure stands of which are uncongenial for a rich and diversified avifauna. Different species of birds are adapted for feeding in different niches on a wide variety of forest insects – wood-boring beetles, defoliating caterpillars, termites, and so on. These infest every part of a tree-root, stem, bark, leaves, flowers, and fruit. Therefore a diverse community of birds needs to be fostered for the proper monitoring of all these parts.

PART IV

BIRDS AT RISK

"It is very true that we seldom appreciate a blessing until we have lost it"

– Sálim Ali, Radio Talks, "Birds: A National Asset" (1941)

The Convention on Wetlands of International Importance especially as Waterfowl Habitat is agreed by representatives of 18 nations, 2 February 1971.

At the first meeting of the Ramsar Convention in 1971 at Ramsar, Iran.

On camel back over the Rann of Kutch salt marsh.

1

The Preservation of Wild Birds*

WITH THE GROWING realisation in Europe and America of the important part that birds play in the affairs of mice and men, an organisation known as the International Committee for Bird Preservation was set up in 1922 with the object of co-ordinating the work of the various bird protection societies that had come into being in many countries, and ensuring the fullest co-operation amongst them. Its revised Declaration of Principles reads as follows:

> We believe that wild bird life is of great importance in the world in helping to preserve the balance between species which Nature is constantly seeking to adjust, that birds have a great importance for science, exercise a great aesthetic influence on all right-minded people, and are of great value to mankind as food, destroyers of rodents and injurious insects, and as incentives for reasonable field sports. We believe that through ignorance, selfishness, and from an undue desire for gain, mankind is reducing the number of birds in many countries at an alarming rate, having in fact exterminated from earth various interesting and valuable species.
>
> We are in sympathy with all reasonable methods to increase the number of game birds in order that the surplus may be used for food

*18 October 1955, Bombay.

or sport. We commend the study of the food habits of wild birds in relation to agriculture, horticulture and forestry, and the publication of information thus obtained, in order that the people of the world may acquire a more accurate conception of the value of bird life.

We rejoice in all efforts being made by educational institutions of whatever nature, as well as by thousands of private individuals, in imparting to the general public knowledge regarding the appearance, habits, activities, and songs of wild birds, so that adults and children alike may be taught to appreciate the aesthetic value of the living bird. We believe that to bring about more adequate bird protection much good can be accomplished by the wider organisation of the International Committee for Bird Preservation . . .

I have thought it worth while to quote this Declaration of Principles in full because it may not be generally known that since 1952 India officially constitutes one of the national sections of the International Committee for Bird Preservation and, as such, has fully endorsed these Principles. It thus becomes incumbent on all of us who are interested in birds to know what the Indian National Section stands for, and to co-operate with it in every possible way for the achievement of its objectives. It may be mentioned here that for administrative convenience the Indian National Section now functions as the so-named Bird Wing of the semi-governmental Indian Board for Wildlife under the Union Ministry of Food and Agriculture.

For a considerable time even before the formation of the International Committee for Bird Preservation, alarm had begun to be felt in the more progressive countries of Europe, and in the U.S.A., over the speed and recklessness with which bird life was being exploited for commercial gain. Particularly alarming did this drain become when prompted and backed by fantastic fashions in women's dress, involving the wholesale use of feathers of wild birds in the millinery trade. The late-Victorian era and the early years of the present century saw a startling devastation of white egrets, whose dainty filmy feathers were in great demand for decorating women's hats and clothes, and for a time almost fetched their weight in gold. Unscrupulous dealers and exporters hired gangs of local hunters to scour the countryside, slaughtering egrets wholesale in order to collect the feathers. The fact that these coveted plumes grow only during the breeding season of the birds, and that they nest in large close-packed heronries, aggravated the matter while adding to the lucrativeness for the operators. These despicable gangs of slaughterers ranged far and wide annihilating heronry after heronry with complete callousness, often killing the parents and leaving the helpless nestlings to starve to death.

Fortunately, in many countries private individuals and unofficial scientific societies were alive to the menace to bird life in the nefarious plumage trade and were ceaselessly campaigning to inform and educate public opinion, and to bring pressure on their governments to stop the senseless extermination. In India it was mainly the persistent efforts and propaganda of the Bombay Natural History Society that brought into being the Wild Birds and Wild Animals Protection Act of 1912. This helped to put a stop to the trade in egret and other wild birds' feathers, and to rehabilitate in some measure the former status of these beautiful and useful creatures. Never before had such a bold and constructive official step been taken in India for the preservation of wild birds. The next comprehensive and progressive measure in the direction of bird preservation, namely the Bombay Wild Animals and Wild Birds Protection Act of 1951, also owes its existence largely to the initiative of the Bombay Natural History Society. This is acknowledged as a model act of its kind and has been commended as such to other states of the Indian Union desirous of introducing similar legislation. Unfortunately even the new Bombay Act is somewhat vitiated by permitting the unrestricted destruction of Birds of Prey as vermin and shows how hard prejudices die. As I mentioned in my previous talk, most hawks and owls, by virtue of their preying so largely on rats and mice, are actually of the greatest benefit to agriculture. It happens to be our good luck that few people in India destroy birds of prey on any extensive scale; therefore no serious depletion need be feared by the time this clause is amended, as it must surely soon be.

As far as direct destruction by man goes, it appears that the current protective legislation is adequate. Thanks to the natural recuperative power of bird species, there is little to fear as long as killing is confined to legitimate sport. The real danger lies in commercialisation. In spite of the sound legislation, we must guard ceaselessly against any form of commercial exploitation of wild birds and smuggling abroad of prohibited feathers by unscrupulous businessmen, particularly through foreign pockets like Goa.

Given reasonable protection, especially during the breeding season, the normal recuperative capacity of wild birds is adequate for replacing normal losses. On the question of preservation there is no occasion for sentimentality, and no reason at all why properly regulated revenue-producing sport should be denied, or people deprived of an occasional roast partridge or quail that has been taken under a legitimate netting licence. While the protection of wild birds is well cared for by the excellent legislation, though perhaps less satisfactorily in the practical administration of the laws, a far greater problem, to my mind, lies in the sphere of habitat conservation. The greatest danger to wild birds of a less adaptable nature and narrowly restricted environments lies not so much in deliberate direct persecution by man as in the elimination, through human interference, of their specialised habitats. Usually it is a combination of these two factors that spells the speedy doom of the more conservative species. A case in point is our Great Indian Bustard which has now – perhaps rather late in the day – been put on the list of totally protected birds. This large and handsome bird, in some ways reminiscent of a miniature ostrich, was tolerably common on the Deccan plains as recently as the commencement of the present century. Its numbers are now dwindling fast all over its range, and the bird is seriously threatened with extinction. This is perhaps due as much to increasing population pressure and the encroachment of its natural habitat by cultivation and the deprivation of suitable breeding areas, as to direct human persecution, the bird's greatest misfortune being that it is bulky in size and at the same time good to eat! Jeeps and modern firearms of course help to hasten the pace of extermination.

Despite the total legislative ban on the killing of the Great Indian Bustard, it seems doubtful if it can be saved from going the way of the Dodo unless adequate tracts of the appropriate country are set apart as sacrosanct refuges where it can live and breed in comparative freedom from disturbance and molestation.

Our resident Pinkheaded Duck appears to have vanished completely within the last forty years or so. Its numbers were never large in recorded history and probably the species was already on the decline a hundred years ago. It is a natural law that when for any reason a wild species reaches a low threshold of numbers, it is often impossible to rehabilitate it by artificial protective measures. The most we can do is to delay its total disappearance. Therefore, it is essential to begin action before it is too late. And in the case of many of our interesting species that means NOW.

That paradise of waterbirds, the Keoladeo Ghana of Bharatpur, to which I referred in the previous talks in this series, is also a habitat which is dependent for its existence as a magnificent heronry entirely upon the supply of water the lake receives at the appropriate season in which the birds nest. Since the change in the political status of Bharatpur State, there have, for a number of reasons, arisen some doubts and uncertainties and conflicts in regard to the availability of this water, which is alleged to be required elsewhere for agricultural purposes. The Bird Wing of the Indian Board for Wildlife is greatly exercised over the outcome, and is striving to get Keoladeo established as a permanent National Waterbird Refuge in order to ensure its continuance for the benefit of future generations of naturalists and bird lovers.

To afford reasonable protection to migratory species, such as most of our wild ducks and geese, which have very widely separated summer and winter quarters involving passage through many intervening countries, the function of international conventions made through national delegates at the annual conferences, and the importance of the International Committee for Bird Preservation become obvious. For instance, Canada might complain, as it has done, that in winter the United States shoots all the ducks that have bred in Canada in spring and summer. For years there has been a persistent allegation, apparently unfounded, that the U.S.S.R. was utilising the yolk of wild ducks' eggs on a large scale in the manufacture of raw cinematograph film, thereby reducing the number of ducks that migrated to other European and Asiatic countries in winter. Prevention of oil pollution of coastal waters by oil-burning ships, which causes great mortality among sea birds, and the reciprocal import and export restrictions on wild bird feathers are two more of the many points in the preservation of birds that have a distinct international bearing. And the International Committee for Bird Preservation with delegates from all the countries concerned is the only organisation that can satisfactorily deal with all such problems.

2

The "Bird Wing" and Bird Preservation in India*

THERE SEEMS LITTLE exaggeration in the claim of persons competent to express the view that life on earth would still go on should Man, by some stroke of poetic justice, suddenly cease to be, but that it would certainly become impossible were birds removed from the scene. In the absence of birds the strict biological check they exercise on insect numbers would disappear and the earth would be overrun by the hungry hordes who, by destroying all vegetation, would soon turn the land into one vast desert.

I said "poetic justice" deliberately because with all the warped genius he is expending on the invention of satanic devices like the hydrogen bomb for use against his fellows, Man is clearly drifting towards the brink of the abyss which will most assuredly engulf him in the end. But even apart from hydrogen bombs and such-like contraptions of the devil, the short-sighted and criminally wasteful way in which he is exploiting his natural resources cannot but lead to his inevitable end within measurable time, unless the forces of destruction are halted before it is too late. In other words the time to halt this vicarious process of self-

*6 October 1956, Bombay.

annihilation is NOW. In the long catalogue of Man's misdeeds and errors of omission and commission, an item of very vital significance is his wanton and thoughtless destruction of forests and the wildlife which goes with them. The importance of wildlife in human ecology and survival is happily being more and more realised and appreciated, and some of the more advanced countries of the world are already making considerable strides in the effective protection and preservation of their indigenous faunas. The International Union for the Protection of Nature, a body sponsored by UNESCO, has been active during the past few years and has done a great deal to dispel apathy and arouse public interest in many countries, and in helping and encouraging national bodies having similar aims and objects with advice and technical assistance. The recent action of the Government of India in constituting the quasi-official Indian Board for Wildlife has been timely and not a day too soon. If it receives the support and co-operation that is its due from state governments and the public, one may confidently look forward to an improvement in the overall situation and to the saving from extinction of many species of indigenous fauna that are in rapid decline due either to thoughtless direct persecution or direct interference by humans. A couple of years even before the formation of the Indian Board for Wildlife the Government of India had been persuaded, largely by representations made to it by the International Committee for Bird Preservation, to constitute the National Committee for India for Bird Preservation affiliated to the international body. With the coming into being of the Central Board of Wildlife to deal with fauna protection in general, this committee ceased to function separately and it now forms a wing of the Board known as the Bird Wing.

Among the two major achievements the Bird Wing can claim – or more correctly near-achievements, since some of the loose threads that still remain to be finally gathered in, are (1) affording sanctuary to that large and handsome bird, the Flamingo, on its traditional breeding ground in the trackless salt marshes of the Great Rann of Kutch, and (2) the conversion of the famous duck-shooting *jheel* of Rajasthan, the Keoladeo Ghana or Bharatpur, into a sanctuary for breeding waterbirds.

The Flamingo, known in Hindi as *Bōg-hans* or *Rāj-hans*, and in Kutchhi as *Hanj*, is, as many may know, a long-legged, long-necked bird standing about 4 ft high to the top of its crown. It lives in flocks, sometimes quite large ones, which feed in the soft mud at the edge of brackish creeks and lagoons, and in salt pans and salt lakes, often in a heavy concentration of brine. Its handsome black-bordered bright crimson wings present a picture of extraordinary beauty as a flock wings its way in a wavy ribbon across the sunset sky or over the dark-grey water, the long neck stretched out in front and the long pink legs trailing stiffly behind. The flamingo was not known to nest in India until some sixty years ago, when the late Maharao Khengarji first discovered its breeding grounds in the remote expanses of the Great Rann. No other breeding colonies have been found in India since. The Rann breeding colony is perhaps the second recorded in Asia, and it has the further distinction of being possibly the largest in the world. Flamingo nests are mounds of mud in the form of an inverted cone about 8" to 14" high, truncated at the top and with a pan-like depression for the egg – normally a singleton. The nests are built close together, averaging more than one to the square yard. When investigated in 1945, the Rann colony – or "Flamingo City" as it is aptly called – covered an area of some 100,000 square yards with a population estimated at about half a million birds. Since the change in the political status of Kutch, conditions had become less happy for the birds, partly due to natural causes such as a succession of drought years, and partly to the removal of protection which the birds previously enjoyed from the game preservation department of erstwhile rulers who were keenly interested in wildlife. Owing to the remoteness of the breeding grounds, and the difficulties of access to them, it had become increasingly difficult to obtain reliable information concerning the Kutch flamingos after the disbandment of the former game department staff. Latterly it had also begun to be alleged that the new embankment across the Little Rann for the Kandla-Deesa railway line was obstructing the outflow of the monsoon waters of several Gujarat rivers into the Great Rann, thereby leaving the former breeding grounds high and dry and unusable by the birds. As the loss of this magnificent colony would have been nothing short of calamitous from the point of view of Indian fauna, the Bird Wing undertook to ascertain the facts on the spot and to devise, if necessary, suitable measures to meet the situation. The investigation turned out a great success not only in disproving the allegation that the railway bund had any deleterious effect on flamingo breeding, but also in procuring definite evidence that, after the good monsoon rains of 1955, the flamingos were in fact breeding in large numbers in the Great Rann. At the same time the enquiry disclosed the disturbing fact that villagers on the borders of the Rann had commenced the practice of rounding up and slaughtering flightless young flamingos in large numbers for food. The Bird Wing was able to initiate prompt action to curb this vandalism by persuading the Kutch Government to appoint a flamingo warden – a local man familiar with the location of the breeding grounds and habits of the birds – who would keep the authorities informed of seasonal flamingo movements and also detect and report to the police the activities of poachers.

In a season of normal rainfall the Keoladeo Ghana of Bharatpur is a veritable paradise for nesting waterbirds such as storks, ibises, cormorants, darters, spoonbills, herons, and egrets. A visit to this gigantic densely populated heronry at the proper time of year is an experience for which a bird lover would gladly travel half round the world – and he would not be disappointed. As an attraction for tourists as well as for scientific naturalists and bird photographers the place holds potentialities of the highest order. Its situation and easy accessibility from the main tourist centres of Delhi and Agra add considerably to its other natural advantages. This natural depression, about 7000 acres in extent, is patchily forested with babul, *Prosopis*, and enormous *kadamb* trees which become partially submerged in the monsoon. The tops of the smaller trees then stand out like little islets above the water and provide ideal sites for waterbirds' nests, which cover the branches thickly, cheek by jowl, often fifty or more clustered together belonging to five or six different species. In former days Keoladeo was the private, carefully guarded duck-shooting preserve of the rulers of Bharatpur, but since the change of the old order the lake had fallen into jeopardy. The popular government planned to drain the bed, cut down the forest, and bring the entire area under permanent cultivation. Repeated representations and agitation by the Bird Wing have fortunately succeeded in saving this unique show-place for posterity. Negotiations are under way for getting the place established by statute as a National Waterbird Sanctuary so that it may continue to be enjoyed by generations of our countrymen and foreign visitors alike. The Flamingo Sanctuary of Kutch and the Waterbird Sanctuary of Bharatpur are two of the major achievements of the Bird Wing. It is to be hoped that they are merely the beginning of a chain of wildlife sanctuaries that will extend throughout the length and breadth of the land to afford protection to the vanishing wealth of fauna and flora with which the country has been blessed by Nature, and which is being subjected to such thoughtless misuse and prodigal waste by its citizens.

3

The Vanishing Species*

THERE ARE, AT THE present time, five species of Indian birds which must unfortunately be considered as well on the road to rapid disappearance, if indeed some of them are not already extinct. In this latter category come the Pink-headed Duck, the Mountain Quail, and Jerdon's Courser. The other two, namely the Great Indian Bustard and the Whitewinged Wood Duck, stand precariously on the danger line, and unless we can put into action immediate and effective measures for their protection, they too will soon be gone.

To maintain the stability of a population, whether animal or plant, it is a law of nature that a certain minimum threshold of numbers is essential so that under normal conditions the increase through breeding is sufficient to counterbalance the losses suffered through disease, enemies, and other natural causes. Once a species crosses this minimum threshold owing to abnormal influences like epidemics, weather, and human interference – whether direct as by excessive killing, or indirect as by destroying its natural habitat – that species may be considered doomed. But it can be saved and even rehabilitated in some measure by wise protective action taken in good time; or at least its continuance may be prolonged

*22 April 1957, Bombay (assumed).

by a process akin to artificial respiration. Under untampered natural conditions the balance is automatically maintained by the struggle for existence.

Let us take the case of the Pinkheaded Duck. Known in Hindi as *Gūlāb-sīr*, it is about the size of the domestic duck, blackish brown overall with a quite distinctive bright rose-pink face, head, and hind neck. This colour has been well likened to that of new blotting paper. A white patch on the wings is conspicuous in flight. The known habitat of this unique non-migratory duck was the swampy jungles of the Terai and Duars along the base of the Himalayas from Oudh and Nepal to Assam, Manipur, and Burma. Out of the breeding season, i.e. in the winter months, it wandered somewhat farther afield. But throughout its recorded history it was never a common or abundant species. Even as early as 1878 the reduction in its numbers drew comment, and it appears to have been steadily on the decline. In the first quarter of the present century, for instance, no more than a couple of dozen specimens were recorded among the hundreds of thousands of duck killed by sportsmen in areas of Bihar and W. Bengal which were its best-known haunts in former days. During the past forty years no reliable record of the occurrence of the Pinkheaded Duck has been received, and in spite of offers of large rewards all efforts to rediscover the species have ended in failure. Probably the very last living examples were the eleven birds that I was fortunate enough to see in the aviaries of Sir Alfred Ezra in London in the early part of 1930. The owner had procured them through his brother the well-known aviculturist of Calcutta, Sir David Ezra, and are believed to have come from the Goalpara District in the extreme west of Assam. In spite of all efforts, no more specimens or authentic records have been forthcoming from that area or elsewhere, and it does seem that we may finally have to reconcile ourselves to the lamentable fact that the bird is extinct. However, as a blanket measure the Government of India, on the recommendation of the Bird Wing of the Indian Board for Wildlife have completely banned the killing of this duck on the forlorn chance that small numbers may possibly still persist in remote areas as yet untouched by drainage and colonisation schemes. In wildlife preservation, it is always a sound principle to protect when in doubt until the necessity for protection is disproved. The classical rediscoveries in recent years of Notornis, the flightless bird of the Rail family of New Zealand, and the Cahow, a petrel (sea bird) of the Bermudas, long considered to be extinct, underline the wisdom of such a policy.

It is incumbent on all sportsmen and others who have the opportunity and are familiar with the appearance of the Pinkheaded Duck and the other vanishing species, either through pictures or museum specimens, to pass on to the Indian Board for Wildlife any dependable information or evidence they may come across, so that a proper scientific investigation may be undertaken by the competent agencies. It is only when we possess definite information regarding the existence, even in small numbers, of species now believed to be extinct or in danger, that specific action can be taken for their protection and preservation.

Several recent reports of the sighting of the Pinkheaded Duck in its former homelands in Bengal and Bihar have, upon closer investigation, proved to refer to the Redheaded Pochard known to shikaris as *Lal-sir* or *Lal-chonch*. This is a migratory species, widely distributed in India during winter, which figures commonly in sportsmen's bags of duck. To avoid some excusable confusion between these two species by casual observers, it may be pointed out that its fluffy mop-like crested head is rich reddish or orange-brown, not blotting-paper pink. Its body is not so wholly blackish brown. In addition to a similar white patch on the wing it has another on the shoulders, as well as a good deal of white on the sides of the body (flanks).

From all that we know, it seems clear that the decline and virtual if not actual extinction of the Pinkheaded Duck is due chiefly to some un-understood natural causes and not to human persecution direct or indirect. It has never been subjected to excessive killing or netting within recent times, and there are still thousands of square miles of suitable swampy jungle left in its former known habitat.

What is perhaps the very opposite of the case of the Pinkheaded Duck, and taking place under our very eyes today, is the rapid disappearance from nearly all areas of its former abundance of the magnificent ground bird, the Great Indian Bustard, known in Hindi as *Tuqdar* or *Hookna*. This bird has the general look of a small ostrich; it stands between 3 and 4 ft high to the top of its head and weighs between 20 and 40 lb. It is deep buffy brown above, white below with a broad black band or gorget across the lower breast, and a black crested crown. The favourite habitat of the Great Indian Bustard is semi-desert country and sparsely scrubbed plains interspersed with patches of cultivation. In the recent past it was widely distributed in peninsular India, especially on the wide Deccan plains, and was even fairly abundant locally. A total of 961 birds are recorded to have been shot by a single shikari between 1809 and 1829 in the Ahmednagar neighbourhood. It was then common also in Mysore, where nowadays it is something of an event to see a bustard.

This spectacular bird, whose nearest relations are found in Africa on the one hand and in Australia on the other, is at present seriously threatened with extinction. Several factors are conspiring towards this end. The high cost of bazaar meat, the increasing human population pressure upon its erstwhile remote haunts, and last but not least the ubiquitous Jeep which enables its quick and easy pursuit by unscrupulous poachers over country which afforded it some immunity in the days on the bullock cart. Added to the despoiling of its breeding grounds is the fact that it is a slow breeder, laying a single egg at a time. And it is amongst the major misfortunes of the bustard that it is bulky in size and good to eat.

The Great Indian Bustard and its eggs are now totally protected by law, but in spite of this there is no doubt that for want of sufficient vigilance on the part of the authorities concerned, and lack of special protective personnel, a great deal of illicit killing of the bird still goes on. We have thus arrived at a stage where perhaps practically all we can expect to achieve is to put off the evil day of its complete disappearance. To my mind the conservation of the bustard's habitat is perhaps even more important than protecting individual birds, and with the vast agricultural development and colonisation schemes under way in all parts of the country it seems doubtful if the bustard can eke out much longer except perhaps in small numbers under careful protection in National Parks.

There are two other Indian birds which, like the Pinkheaded Duck, one does not know whether to write off as already extinct or optimistically to retain on the list of species in imminent danger. Both of them have only been rarely and erratically met with in the past, and practically nothing of their ecology and history is known. Specimens that can be counted on less than the fingers of two hands, now dispersed in some of the world's great natural-history museums abroad, is all the evidence we possess. Recent special expeditions and prolonged search in the areas where they were originally discovered have yielded no clue to their existence, and the complete legislative ban on their killing may prove to be meaningless. These two birds are the Mountain Quail from the Mussoorie–Nainital area of the Western Himalayas at 5000 to 7000 ft, and Jerdon's Courser, a bird of scrubby plains country originally described from Andhra state whose nearest relatives now live in Africa.

Why these birds have remained so completely lost during the

last fifty to seventy-five years since they were first discovered is a complete mystery.

The fifth bird on our danger list, or one at least that needs cautious watching, is the Whitewinged Wood Duck, a resident of the swampy grass jungles and *jheels* of E. Pakistan, Assam, and Burma – a habitat similar to that of the Pinkheaded Duck. It is a large duck usually seen in pairs blackish above, rusty below, with a broad white shoulder patch and black-speckled white head and neck. In overall effect it resembles the more familiar Nukta or Comb Duck. This duck has never been reported as plentiful, and is now rarely seen even in its typical habitat. But, as a precaution against its going the way of the Pinkheaded Duck, its killing is banned by law, and the question of rehabilitating it artificially in some of the areas where it was found in the recent past is engaging the attention of the Bird Wing.

4

The Flamingo*

ONE OF THE ornithological highlights of India, which may well be the pardonable envy of less fortunate countries, is the unique nest-city of the Flamingo in the Great Rann of Kutch. At the height of the breeding season, when in full occupation, acres of the desolate, featureless landscape are transformed into one seething mass of white and crimson with tens of thousands of these large and spectacular birds sitting on their eggs or standing about amongst the plum-pudding mounds of mud which are their nests. The babel of their goose-like honking and the incessant traffic to and fro of the foraging bands fill the air by day and by night (like some mighty electric generator at work in the distance).

For the benefit of such as may be somewhat hazy in their minds as to what I am talking about, it may be mentioned that the flamingo is a large, tall, stork-like bird standing about 4 ft to the top of its head, of rosy-white plumage with long, bare strawberry-coloured legs, and a slender coiling neck. Its peculiar heavy pink bill, turned down angularly for half its length, leaves no excuse whatever for confusing it with any other similar bird. In flight the black-bordered brilliant scarlet wings present a spectacle

*9 July 1957, Bombay.

of exquisite charm. Indeed a flock of flamingos against the sunset sky, flying in wavy diagonal ribbons or orderly wedge formation, is a sight that is not easily forgotten. During the non-breeding season the birds disperse far and wide over the peninsula and it is a reasonable presumption that large numbers from the Kutch colony even migrate to East Africa then. Actual proof of this, however, like in so many other flamingo problems, can only come through large-scale marking of the birds and adequate follow-up.

Even in localities which constitute their normal feeding haunts, their appearances are erratic since the degree of salinity necessary for the production of their special food varies locally from year to year depending upon the rainfall. Their diet consists of vegetable matter and minute or even microscopic organisms (copepods, diatoms) scooped up in the inverted bill along with liquid mud and brine from the bottom of salt marshes, and strained through a special filtering device. The large fleshy tongue which aids in this process fills the mouth cavity and precludes the swallowing of large food. Though sometimes found at freshwater *jheels*, they are essentially frequenters of salt or brackish water and oftener met with on tidal creeks and coastal lagoons. Inland, the Sambhar Salt Lake of Rajasthan is one of their best-known permanent haunts in the non-breeding season.

Altogether five species of flamingo are recognised throughout the world. Three of these are confined to the New World, the remaining two being found in Europe, Africa, and Asia. The smaller of these two, known as the Lesser Flamingo, breeds most abundantly in Africa but is also suspected to do so in the Little Rann of Kutch where enormous concentrations are regularly seen, including young birds of the year. Actual nesting within Indian limits has not been proved. Uptil 1893, when the Great Rann colony was first discovered by the late Maharao Shri Khengarji, the best-known breeding grounds of the larger Old World species were the delta of the Guadalquivir River in Spain and the salt marshes of the Camargue in southern France, where, in general, the ecological conditions are rather similar to those in the Rann. From recent investigations, it appears that the Kutch colony is perhaps the largest and most populous of all the ones known. The regular breeding grounds ("Flamingo City") lie some seven or eight miles out in the midst of the Great Rann which separates Kutch from Sind. This vast expanse of billiard table flatness (*ca.* 21,500 sq. km – *ca.* 320 km long × 160 wide, max.), is covered for the most part with a dirty-looking squelchy ooze underlying a shallow crust of concentrated brine, or thickly encrusted dark silt, as far as the eye can reach, with salt crystals that crunch and splinter like glass under the horses' hooves and take on, under the scorching sun, the blinding glare and whiteness of a snowfield.

The colony can be reached either on ponies or on camels, a form of slithering nerve-racking transport which I strongly do not recommend, in about two and a half hours from the nearest point on Pachcham Island.

A pony ridden out and back a couple of times over this razor-edged salt encrustation becomes lame and virtually useless for the next two or three days, adding greatly to the problems of transport and other *bandobast* in this godforsaken place.

In the 1945 nesting season the number of birds in the Rann colony, including adults and young, was calculated to be of the order of half a million. On a visit to the place last April, the number of nests which the young birds had very recently vacated was determined, by means of sample area-counts, to be between 125 and 150 thousand. This would imply a population of 2½ to 3 lakhs of adults and, on a conservative reckoning, about 2 lakh young, thus independently agreeing with the earlier estimate.

The most important requirement of the flamingo for successful breeding in the Great Rann seems to be a certain optimum shallowness of water covering the nest site during the appropriate period. This condition is largely dependent on the S.W. Monsoon, both directly by the rainfall and indirectly by the discharge of the flood waters of the Luni and smaller rivers of Rajasthan into it. If the rainfall has been heavy, the water at the nest site is too deep for the building of new nests or the repair of old ones. If the monsoon has been scanty, the nest site remains high and dry and is then equally unusable. In addition, it is also of primary importance that the requisite water conditions should coincide with the nesting season of the birds and it is perhaps to allow for this that the breeding season in Kutch, at any rate, is so uncommonly elastic and prolonged. The birds here seem capable of nesting at short notice any time between September/October and March/April, therefore during well over half the year!

The nest of the flamingo is a conical mound of sun-baked clayey mud, scraped from the vicinity and piled up when in a semi-liquid state. It is truncated at the top and with a flat, shallow pan-like depression, or crater, for the egg. The mounds vary in height from almost flush with the ground to 18 to 20 inches, and are built in clusters, sometimes several thousand together, covering many acres of ground and justifying the name "flamingo city" by which they are collectively known. Usually a single egg is laid, rarely two, of the size and appearance of a goose's egg.

During a recent run of three or four drought years, apparently no nesting took place in the Rann though the birds were observed to collect there at the appointed time. It began to be alleged that the new embankment for the Kandla-Dessa railway across the head of the Little Rann was cutting off the outflow of the monsoon waters from N. Gujarat and Rajasthan into the Great Rann, and inhibiting the water conditions needed by the birds. This allegation, if true, would indeed have meant a catastrophe for India from the ornithological point of view, and it caused much perturbation among bird lovers. The Bird Wing of the Indian Board for Wildlife at once took up the matter and conducted an on-the-spot investigation. It was happily proved beyond a doubt that the bund had nothing to do with the non-breeding of flamingos in the years in question, but that the failures were due purely to deficient monsoons. It is a well-known fact in all parts of the world, wherever flamingos breed, that successful large-scale nesting takes place on an average only once in two or three years due to a variety of unpropitious natural causes. In some years the nesting may be greatly reduced, while in others it may be completely inhibited. The puzzle is: what happens to the birds physiologically ready to breed, but who do not find the requisite natural conditions? Are they capable of skipping a season altogether or do they migrate elsewhere to seek alternative grounds? The latter possibility has been suggested for Kutch flamingos in a year of drought. It has even been hinted that there may actually be a regular two-way traffic, flamingos from the European and African breeding colonies migrating to Kutch in unfavourable years, and vice versa. This problem again can only be solved through large-scale marking of the birds in the various colonies.

Happily, the Kutch flamingo has few enemies. The remoteness and comparative inaccessibility of its breeding grounds is its most effective natural safeguard, not only against four-footed predators but also against the arch-enemy, Man. But although its remoteness and the sparsity of the non-vegetarian population in the surrounding areas make the colony safe from commercial egg-gatherers, who are the bane of European and American colonies, a considerable amount of destruction of flightless young birds does take place after they leave the nest city and are escorted to their feeding grounds within easier reach of man. The meat-hungry villagers along the edge of the Rann round up and slaughter the helpless young, which on account of the thick layer of fat covering them at this period are particularly relished as food. In order to check this destructive practice, the Forest Department has been persuaded to engage a knowledgeable local as "flamingo guard", and when the Bombay Wild Animals and Wild Birds Protection Act of 1951 becomes applicable to Kutch, it is hoped to intensify the measures for the protection of the bird. However, it can happily be claimed as perhaps for no other large Indian wild animal or bird at the present time, that the position of the flamingo is safe, and it stands in no danger of extinction through avoidable man-made causes. But looking to current trends, it seems certain that this happy state of affairs can not endure unless the natural protection it enjoys is fortified by adequate statutory protection; in other words by the establishment, without delay, of the Kutch breeding grounds as a National Flamingo Sanctuary.[‡]

[‡]Two handwritten jottings on the typed script – the second partially illegible on account of punches on the paper – which were not a part of the talk and noted at a later date – read as follows: "*P. minor* discovered breeding among Flamingo City, Gt. Rann, Jan. 1974, for first time." And: ". . . *ruber* breeds . . . Kazakhstan . . . the Caspian Region. Also in . . . Afghanistan (Ab-e istadeh)." – Ed.

5

Some Endangered Waterbirds of Assam*

OF THE 2000 FORMS of birds found in the subcontinent of India together with Pakistan, some 350 are winter visitors chiefly from Europe and Asia north of the Himalayas. They commence arriving in the northern areas about September, spread themselves out over the Peninsula by November, and are mostly gone again by the middle of April. Northern birds migrate to southern countries in order to escape the rigours of winter – low temperatures, scarcity of food both vegetable and animal, and short daylight hours of feeding. They return to their homelands in spring when conditions again become favourable with sufficient warmth, food, and daylight for bringing up their families. Students of bird migration believe that when crossing high mountain ranges, migrating birds prefer to fly along the courses of rivers rather than directly across the mountains and in this way they minimise the hazards of the journey – storms, blizzards, and unfavourable weather. Thus, to cross over into India from the north they are supposed to avoid the mighty Himalayan barrier by working down the Indus Valley in the west and the Brahmaputra Valley in the east, which form gaps at either end

*4 July 1964, Bombay, for broadcast from Gauhati.

of the mountain chain. Mounting evidence provided by recent mountaineering expeditions in the Himalayas and investigations by means of radar in Europe and America indicate that this notion is not altogether correct. Birds are shown to be capable of flying at enormous heights without physical inconvenience, and they do so without any apparent compulsion. The river valley hypothesis is probably largely true in the case of ducks and many other waterbirds since it provides them with favourable opportunities for resting and feeding as they gradually work their way up or down to their seasonal quarters.

The Brahmaputra Valley, through which flows this mighty river and its numerous tributaries, abounds in numerous low-lying swamps or *jheels* created by the monsoon spillage, and provides particularly attractive living conditions for waterbirds. In addition to the numerous resident birds which live and breed within the country throughout the year, the abundance and variety of the migratory waterbirds that make their appearance here between the months of September and April is truly impressive. Discriminating sportsmen frequently find rare and unlikely exotic N.E. Asian species among their bags of waterfowl, and there seems no limit to what may turn up now and then. Unfortunately duck-shooters as a tribe seldom bother to examine their bags intelligently to find out what they have shot. All that matters to most is the number of birds they kill and the amount of meat that each bird will produce. In this way a good many interesting records are doubtless lost.

Most of the resident waterbirds of Assam are of course common to other well-watered parts of the Indian Union as well. They include the storks (at least five species), herons, egrets, cormorants, darters, and sparingly also spottedbilled pelicans. There is one species of heron of particular interest since although apparently a resident bird its nest has so far not been found in Assam.

This is the Great Whitebellied Heron. It is a large long-legged long-necked marsh bird, considerably larger than the familiar Grey Heron (*Sardo Koi* in Assamese) but with a slaty black head instead of white, and a glistening white belly. It is not a difficult species to identify in the field once attention is drawn to these points, and it is hoped that listeners will keep a sharp lookout for this bird and find out something about its status and habits which are so little known.

Assam can boast of at least one species of resident wild duck, the Whitewinged Wood Duck, which is found nowhere else within the subcontinent except sparingly in Bangladesh. It lives chiefly in eastern Assam north of the Brahmaputra, in N. Lakhimpur and those parts, being rare and occasional in western Assam, in the Kamrup and Goalpara districts. It keeps in pairs or small parties of half a dozen birds or so, frequenting secluded swamps in deep wet forest away from human habitations. This is a large duck, larger than the domestic species, rather like a Nukta in appearance, especially in its speckled white head and neck. The rest of the plumage, however, is largely glistening black and chestnut brown. A large white patch on the wing, particularly conspicuous in flight, is a good distinguishing mark. The special interest in this duck, known locally as *Deo hans* and in Cachar as *Daophlantu*, lies in its growing scarcity, which is causing concern to wildlife conservationists throughout the world. The causes of the decline are not properly understood since the bird has not been subjected to any undue hunting pressure in the past, and within recent years has been totally protected by law. It is feared that this species may soon follow another very interesting Indian duck, formerly also found in Assam, which has become extinct within the last fifty years. Some of the last Pinkheaded Ducks – a batch of eleven said to have been obtained in Goalpara district – were exported to London in 1929 or thereabouts and lived for several years in captivity there, but all efforts to breed them proved unsuccessful. The last wild Pinkheaded Duck was shot in Bihar in 1935, since when it has vanished completely and all efforts to rediscover it have ended in failure. There is a forlorn hope that possibly a few may still be surviving in some remote and secluded *jheels* in northern Assam, and sportsmen visiting such areas will do well to keep a special lookout for the bird. They may be reminded, however, that this species is completely protected by law and should on no account be killed. It is such a distinctive looking bird that an accurate description by a reasonably experienced birdwatcher or shikari, written down on the spot, should be acceptable evidence. In the male the head and bill and neck are rose pink – the exact colour of fresh pink blotting paper – and the body blackish brown both above and below. In the female the head is merely suffused with the same pink tinge, but less bright. This bird must not be confused with the Redcrested Pochard, as has frequently been done by overenthusiastic but uncritical observers. The latter is a fairly common duck in winter, which has a fluffy golden orange (not pink) head, black breast, and white sides of body.

Yet a third species which deserves special mention among the waterbirds of Assam is the curious Masked Finfoot. Elsewhere within our subcontinental limits this bird is found only in Bangladesh. It belongs to a family closely related to the Rail, and is characterised by a peculiarly splintered distribution, some of its nearest relations being found in Africa and others in America. In general aspect the finfoot, so called because of the lobe-like fringes of skin on its toes, is not unlike a coot. It is larger, chiefly olive-brown above, white below, with a black face and foreneck and a large, prominent, pointed yellow bill. It is shy and lives in remote jungle swamps, seldom showing itself. Its presence, however, is given away by the peculiar high-pitched call resembling the sound made by blowing air through a tube into water. This is another denizen of Assam's swamps regarding whose life history exceedingly little is known. Zoology students of Gauhati University are to be envied for the opportunities they have at their doorstep for the much-neglected field study of the birds of Assam.

PART V

NATURE IN INDIA

"What is now required is the understanding of the fact that human ecology is an integral part of Nature conservation, and all who take a total view of life on earth must realise that man's future cannot be considered separately from that of other life"

– Sálim Ali, Radio Talks, "Man and Nature in India" (1976)

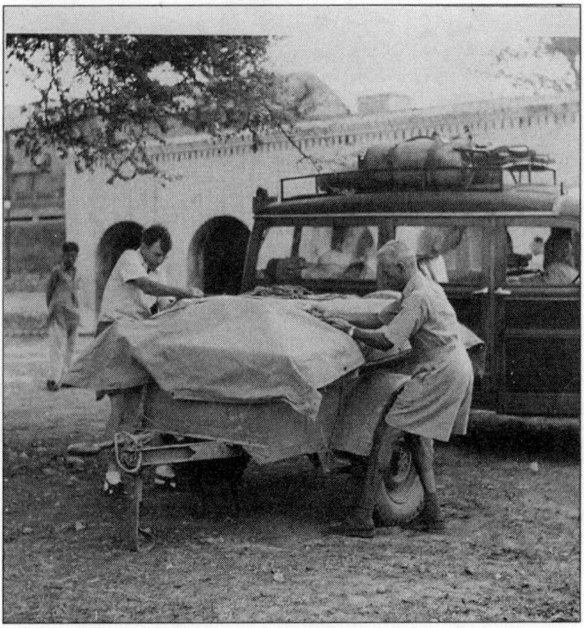

Preparing for a camp in Kashmir, 1951.
(*Photo by Loke Wan Tho.*)

In Sikkim.

1

The Fauna of India*

INDIA IS A LITTLE LESS than two-thirds the size of Europe in area. It covers some 40 degrees of latitude and about the same of longitude. Its far-flung frontiers encompass a great diversity of climatic and physical features, ranging from the scorching sandy deserts of Rajasthan and the humid rain forests of Assam and Travancore to the region of glaciers and eternal snow on the mighty Himalayas.

It is therefore only natural that its fauna should be as rich and varied as it is. We have over 500 different species of mammals and something like 1800 species of birds. And in addition there are of course the reptiles, amphibians, and other animal groups all of equally great variety and interest.

Of the larger and more spectacular mammals the tiger and the elephant are traditionally associated with India in the popular foreign mind. The status they enjoy abroad is perhaps on a par with turbaned mystics and the rope trick, and maharajas with Arabian Nights pageantry.

Besides the tiger, we have from among its cousins the lion, the panther, and the snow leopard. The lion was much more abundant and widespread in India even in fairly recent historical times.

*12 November 1952, Bombay (for the External Service).

Up to a period it was considered nobler game than the tiger and enjoyed great esteem as a trophy of the chase. It appears to have given way gradually in competition with the tiger which is a domiciled in-migrant from its original home in the reedy swamps of Manchuria. At the present time our lion is confined to one small area of Saurashtra known as the Gir Forest, and but for the active reservation by the erstwhile rulers of Junagadh State, the species would have vanished from India completely. About thirty-five years ago its population had dwindled to well under thirty individuals. With stringent protection it has increased, and the latest census taken in 1949/50 revealed that there were in all something like 225 animals living in the Gir area.

For all the claims made on its behalf, the Indian lion does not differ appreciably from its African counterpart nor for that matter is our leopard – more commonly known as panther in India – different from the African. The Cheetah or Hunting Leopard, now virtually extinct in India, is also the same animal as found in Africa. The mammals of India and Africa provide an interesting comparison. While Africa abounds in antelopes and gazelles of which we have but few species here, it lacks the true Deer, such as our magnificent Kashmir Stag and our beautiful Sambar and Cheetal, with the exception of a single species on the shores of the Mediterranean. Africa is also completely devoid of Bears, of which we possess at least three species.

Under the statutory protection it enjoys, the Indian Elephant has of late increased greatly in numbers. In some parts of South India it is now by way of becoming a serious menace to cultivation. Since a full-grown elephant will consume something like 700 lb. per day in leaves and grass, it can be realised what enormous destruction a herd may cause to crops in a single night, particularly as in milling around the great beasts trample down almost more than they actually eat. With the decline of princely pageantry in modern India and increasing mechanisation for haulage and such heavy work, much of the elephant's former usefulness is lost. In some parts of the country it has now become a problem how to control its numbers. Bull elephants, moreover, occasionally turn rogue and become a terror to the entire countryside, wantonly tearing down cultivators' huts, destroying crops and plantations, and chasing down and killing humans with fiendish cunning and determination.

The Indian One-horned Rhinoceros is probably the largest surviving representative of its tribe. A bull stands over 5½ ft high at the shoulder. Its present habitat is the belt of swampy tall grass jungle which stretches along the base of the Himalayas from Nepal to Assam. Its numbers had dwindled alarmingly in the last hundred years owing to the lucrative demand from China for its blood and horn which are believed to possess medicinal and rejuvenating properties. The animal has of late been completely protected by law and its numbers are slowly but steadily on the increase. In spite of some desultory poaching that still continues, the Indian rhino is happily in no immediate danger of extinction, thanks particularly to the special sanctuaries formed for its preservation in Bengal and Assam. Its overall population was estimated in 1949 by experts of the Bombay Natural History Society not to exceed 500 individuals.

The Kaziranga Wildlife Sanctuary of Assam is perhaps the most convenient place for seeing the Indian rhinoceros in its wild state. It is easy of access and provides facilities for halting as well as trained riding elephants from which to view and photograph the animal. This sanctuary also contains other interesting forms of animal life including wild buffalo, swamp deer, florican, and the rare whitewinged wood duck.

The Gaur or so-called Indian Bison, another spectacular denizen of the Indian jungles, enjoys the distinction of being the world's largest wild ox. A good bull stands 6ft 4in. at the shoulder and weighs over 2000 lb. Mysore and Travancore in South India are the main strongholds of the Gaur at present, and it is also not uncommon in some of the Assam hill forests. In spite of its forbidding massiveness the Gaur is an inoffensive forest animal. It shuns the proximity of man and does little damage to cultivation. Except when wounded by a sportsman it is not dangerous, though an encounter at close quarters when armed with nothing more deadly than a camera is likely to provide all the thrill that any sportsman can desire. That thrill, moreover, may be increased by the knowledge that on rare occasions soured old bulls are not unknown to charge without provocation!

For majestic grandeur the Kashmir Stag or Hanglu stands undisputed leader of our numerous and beautiful Deer tribe. It inhabits the forests of Kashmir, moving up and down the mountains seasonally between 5000 and 14,000 ft altitude. Recent disturbed conditions had brought about a great depletion in its numbers, but the present government are taking active measures for rehabilitation. For among the countless natural attractions of this paradise for the holiday-maker and the sportsman, the Hanglu is by no means a negligible item. The Dachigam Wildlife Sanctuary near Srinagar, situated in superb natural surroundings, is one of the delights that await the visitor to Kashmir in autumn, winter, and early spring when the deer are down in the Valley and the stags in the full glory of their majestic antlers.

Over the rest of the Indian subcontinent two other beautiful deer are common, namely the Sambar or Rusa Deer and the Cheetal or Spotted Deer. The former dwells in dense forest country, the latter favouring a more open type of jungle, especially where interspersed with cultivation. These two, along with the wild pig, form the staple food of tiger and panther, and the carnivores perform a great service in maintaining the balance of nature by keeping their numbers in check. In some jungle areas deer and wild pig do considerable damage to villagers' crops and to young forest plantations of economic timber trees.

With our growing population pressure and the opening up of hitherto remote jungle areas for greater food production it has become a vital matter to devise effective protection for our varied and interesting fauna which is fast losing ground on every front. Fortunately the Government of India, fully realising that our wildlife is a national asset, to be held in trust for future generations, have constituted a Central Board for Wildlife to educate public opinion and advise state government in matters connected with its preservation and the establishment of National Parks. Several excellent sanctuaries already exist in India, notably in Mysore, Travancore, Assam, and Uttar Pradesh. There is an ample fund of latent public goodwill towards wildlife, and scientific bodies like the Bombay Natural History Society, as well as far-sighted individual sportsmen and naturalists are ceaselessly striving for its preservation. It is hoped that there will soon be functioning a chain of well-managed national parks and game reserves where opportunities for the aesthetic enjoyment and scientific study of Indian fauna and flora will be readily available to all, and where facilities for controlled big-game hunting and wildlife photography will compare with the best in the world.

2

Wildlife Preservation in Kashmir*

THE NATURAL ATTRACTIONS of Kashmir as a holiday resort have been justly extolled. Surprisingly enough one important facet of its charm does not appear to have received its due share of appreciation and publicity, and that is its fauna. Yet the rich and varied animal life of Kashmir is of the greatest interest to the visitor and to the naturalist and sportsman in particular. The State lies on the boundary of Eur-Asia, or what is known to students of animal geography as the Palaearctic Region on the one hand, and of the Indian Region south of the great Himalayan mountain barrier on the other. Some of its birds and mammals, as well as plants, are identical with those found in Europe and North Asia and are not met with anywhere else within Indian limits. Two typical example of such are the Jackdaw among birds and the Brown Bear among mammals. The former which is such a familiar bird of the Srinagar Valley is a smaller and more gentlemanly edition of our own House Crow, and has a distinctive pale grey eye. The latter lives high up in the mountains and has to be specially looked for. A large number of birds which are seen in the plains of India only during the winter months migrate northward in spring to Kashmir and neighbouring lands in order to bring up their families. Between April and September the

*17 November 1952, Bombay.

number and variety of birds to be met with in Kashmir are almost overwhelming. For the visitor during that season the advantage is that 90 per cent of the birds he comes across will be busy with their nesting operations – either building nests or sitting on eggs, or else feeding the young. A bird photographer or serious ornithologist can hardly hope to find a pleasanter or more productive field for his activities than Kashmir in springtime and early summer.

Among the larger mammals, Kashmir possesses many species that form coveted trophies for the hunter of big game and which in more settled times had attracted sportsmen from all over the world. Brown and Black Bear and Snow Leopard are amongst the chief attractions. The northern and more rugged portions of the country, like Ladakh, are particularly rich in species of wild goats and sheep including the stately *Ovis ammon*, a good ram of which stands as high as a donkey. The hunting of markhor, ibex, and the *ammon* sheep is an exhilarating though arduous sport that calls not only for fighting fitness of physique in the hunter and great power of endurance, but also for the many other qualities that go with serious mountaineering. These animals live at high altitudes on steep mountainsides and precipices where the ground is all in their favour. The sportsman's success depends entirely upon his own staunchness in wind and limb, and upon his skill as a marksman under the difficult conditions.

But perhaps the most highly prized trophy of all that Kashmir has to offer is the Barasinga or Hanglu. This grand animal is a close relation of the European Red Deer. A good stag stands 48–50 inches at the withers and may weigh over 400 lb. It carries an imposing head of majestically spreading horns usually with between 10 and 14 points. The record horns measure 50½ inches on the outside curve, and heads of up to 45 inches are not uncommon.

The Barasinga was plentiful in the various State Rakhs or Game Preserves of Kashmir up to the time of the recent disturbed conditions. It was carefully preserved, and only controlled shooting of a limited number of mature stags was permitted each year under licences issued by the Game Department.

With the difficult food position and the great rise in the cost of mutton assisted by the general laxness in the administration of law and order which preceded and immediately followed the tribesmen's raid, the Barasinga was poached with impunity everywhere and slaughtered on a commercial scale; and its numbers became sorely depleted.

The present government of Jammu and Kashmir, quick to appraise this unhappy state of affairs, invited the Bombay Natural History Society as the recognised competent authority on wildlife problems, to investigate the matter and make practicable suggestions for the rehabilitation of their various wildlife sanctuaries and in particular for retrieving the position of this beautiful deer.

The representatives who toured the game areas to evaluate the situation have now submitted their report and recommendations to the Kashmir government. It is hoped that they will lead to a steady improvement in the general wildlife position of the state and to the gradual return of the Barasinga to its former abundance.

Apart from the indiscriminate slaughter which has of late been rampant, the deer are also exposed to other and more natural forms of harassment. It is clear, for example that one of the not unimportant contributory causes of their decline is the great increase that has taken place in the population of the Himalayan Black Bear. In normal times bona fide sportsmen and professional fur hunters used to account for a considerable number of black bear annually, thus helping to keep its numbers in check. Of recent years few sportsmen have been visiting Kashmir. Local shikaris and holders of licensed crop-protection guns, and also of numerous illicit firearms, have long discovered that shooting the Barasinga for its meat and hide was a far more lucrative proposition than expending precious powder and shot on the uneatable bear whose skin, moreover, had practically no market value at present.

Barasinga hinds drop their fawns in March/April which roughly coincides with the time the black bear awakens from its winter sleep. The animals have used up their accumulated fat during hibernation and are now lean and particularly ravenous. Though professedly, and to a large extent vegetarian, the black bear is not squeamish about stretching the point and will gladly take to meat when it can be procured. Therefore tender young Barasinga fawns make a welcome addition to its bill of fare, particularly when plant life is not yet in its post-winter primc and its staple food of tubers, fruits, and honey unobtainable. Newly born Barasinga are puny little creatures and remain helpless for several days after birth. At this stage they are highly vulnerable and fall an easy prey to foraging bears, the black as well as the brown. The latter species though less abundant and living at higher altitudes is also destructive to the deer.

Estimates of local shikaris and experienced Game Watchers vary considerably as to the extent of damage caused by the black bear to Barasinga fawns. Some would reckon it as negligible while others place it as high as nine fawns out of ten. The truth doubtless lies in between and must vary with circumstances and in different localities. It is even possible that in normal times the mortality due to bears actually helps to maintain the balance of nature. But times are not normal either as to increase in bears or decrease in Barasinga, and therefore every factor operative towards lowering and holding down Barasinga numbers has to be taken into account. That the black bear has increased greatly in recent years is undisputed – the Dachigam Sanctuary is stiff with them – and this adds to its destructive potentialities.

The virtual decontrol of shooting restrictions due to the erstwhile slackening in the administration, the reduction in the game staff, the profitable and clamant demand for Barasinga meat and the unprecedented increase in guns, both licensed and clandestine, are some of the factors that have contributed to the downfall of this majestic and beautiful deer. What makes matters worse is that, unlike the bear which enjoys virtual immunity from humans during the winter months when it is hibernating in caves and secluded places, the deer is subjected to round-the-year persecution. In summer the Gujars who with their flocks and herds for fresh grazing follow the deer up to the highest Alpine pastures, slay what they can regardless of age or sex; while in autumn and winter when the deer descend to lower levels and are in the full glory of hard horn they receive the attentions not only of licensed sportsmen – for it is then the open shooting season – but also of poaching meat-hunters from the valley.

One of the recommendations of the Bombay Natural History Society's investigators is that the black bear should be officially proclaimed vermin forthwith, and a reward of Rs 15/- offered for the destruction of every animal. Among other measures it is recommended that the game staff be increased, particularly in the Dachigam Sanctuary near Srinagar which serves as the central stock reservoir for Barasinga and supplies the surrounding shooting areas. The salaries of the game staff should be raised to a fair living wage – to a figure in fact where it may be less unreasonable to expect them to remain honest and resist temptation in the shape of bribes offered by poachers and other law breakers.

Last but not least in potential effectiveness is the recommendation that all guns licensed to cultivators specifically for crop protection should be called in at the end of the cultivation season, after the crops have been harvested. This will involve no hardship on the cultivator and no one can reasonably take exception to the measure. In winter there are no crops to protect from wild animals, whereas on the other hand it is just the season when the deer concentrate in the warmer lower valleys in easily accessible areas and are particularly vulnerable to poaching. In as much as these ostensibly "crop protection" guns are responsible for a large proportion of the destruction from which wildlife suffers in Kashmir, as elsewhere in India, it is felt that the withdrawal of guns at a season when there can be no legitimate excuse for their retention should prove of distinct advantage in the preservation of game animals.

In all these various ways it is hoped in due course to restore to Kashmir the glory of her wildlife and particularly the Barasinga or Hanglu which is certainly one of her most spectacular and beautiful natural assets.

3

Some Interesting Animals of Sikkim*

IN THE LAST TWO talks I had occasion to say something about the climate and physiography of Sikkim in general, and about some of the more noteworthy birds to be met with in this peculiarly interesting faunal region. For the benefit of those who missed the previous talks, it seems useful to recapitulate in brief the main physical characteristics of the area in order to provide an intelligible background to its animal life.

The semi-independent state of Sikkim is a vertically oblong wedge of mountainous Himalayan country lying between Nepal on the west and Bhutan on the east. Its southern and south-east boundary runs with the Darjeeling District of West Bengal. On the north and north-east it is bounded by Tibet. On account of its natural position at the head of the Bay of Bengal and athwart the moisture laden winds of the South-West Monsoon, it is perhaps the most humid tract in the entire chain of the Himalayas. It is a country of heavy rainfall and luxuriant vegetation, and on account of its abruptly mountainous nature, rising from about 1000 ft above sea level to peaks of over 20,000 ft within less than thirty miles, it contains a number of well-marked vegetational zones telescoped in it, beginning with tropical and ascending through subtropical and

*10 August 1953, Bombay.

temperate to alpine. The tropical and subtropical zones are marked by the presence of an abundance of epiphytes, and Sikkim includes in its flora some of the most magnificent orchids to be found in the Indian region. The larger trees in the temperate zone are heavily draped in beard-moss which hangs in dense bunches from the boughs, and is often over a foot in length.

A zoological expedition sponsored by the Bombay Natural History Society under my leadership has been exploring in Sikkim during the past winter. The main object of the expedition was to study the birdlife particularly from the ecological standpoint, and to investigate the general life conditions of high-altitude birds forced down to lower elevations by the rigour of the climate during that season. While the material and data collected by the expedition mainly concerned the avifauna, secondary attention was also paid to Mammals and to other groups of animals. In this talk I propose to give a general random account of the animals of Sikkim. "Animals" is here used rather loosely, and in its popularly accepted sense. More correctly it should be Mammals, that is, the warm-blooded class that includes man himself, whose bodies are more or less covered with hair and who suckle their young.

The entire area of which Sikkim forms part is a confused network of valleys and mountains, growing higher and higher and culminating in the majestic snow-clad Kinchinjunga, *ca.* 28,000 ft. The hillsides are excessively steep, and up to an elevation of 7000 ft or so, below the level of conifers, are clothed in dense heavy tropical forest growth with a great abundance of bamboos. The temperate zone is a region of willow, juniper, stunted birch, silver fir, and wild rose with a profusion of dwarf rhododendrons of numerous species.

Sikkim contains two distinct faunas, the Palaearctic to the north and Oriental to the south with a fairly sharp line of demarcation between them at about the 28th N. parallel. The mighty barrier of the

Himalayan range in the north, by shutting India off from the very different climatic conditions prevailing in Central Asia, has helped to conserve its distinct flora and fauna. Typically Palaearctic forms such as the wild sheep Bharal (*Pseudois*), Mole (*Talpa*), Mouse-hare (*Ochotona*) are found in juxtaposition with such typically Oriental species as Flying Fox, Civet Cat, Mongoose, and Giant Squirrel, which all adds to the interest and complexity of the country for the investigating zoologist.

In Sikkim also – more correctly a short distance from its political western boundary, in eastern Nepal – is the meeting point of the Indian and Malayan faunas of the Oriental Region. This condition, observed in the case of birds by the splitting up into east Himalayan and west Himalayan forms, is confirmed by other groups of the animal kingdom as well. Among mammals the various genera of squirrels provide an excellent example. Natural obstacles such as deep gorges, wide rivers, and high mountains present a much more formidable and effective barrier to the distribution of terrestrial animals than of birds. Therefore the evidence deduced from the pattern of geographical distribution of mammals is in many respects more convincing than from birds, which on account of their facility for aerial locomotion are able to overcome obstacles which constitute effective barriers to the spread of mammals. Apart from the so-called Giant Squirrels and Flying Squirrels, the western Himalayas possess only a single genus of squirrels (*Funambulus*), which is also common to the rest of continental and peninsular India. This genus is conspicuously absent in Sikkim, being replaced by several genera characteristic of the eastern Himalayas and Malaysia. On the other hand, several genera of rats, e.g. *Nesokia* found westward of Kumaon, extending thence as far as Iran, the Middle East, and even Egypt, are not found at all east of Kumaon, even in Nepal. The Kali River seems to limit its eastward distribution. When talking on the birds of Sikkim I mentioned the curious parallelism that exists in the general aspect of the fauna and flora between Sikkim, the eastern Himalayas, and Malaysia on the one hand, and the humid heavy rainfall areas of the southern section of the Western Ghats on the other. Several instances of this peculiar broken geographical distribution of similar or identical but specialised forms, separated by over 1000 miles of unsuited country, were given. Such examples are to be found not only in birds, but in other forms of life as well, including the plants.

Among mammals, a good instance of this sort of thing is provided by the Yellowthroated Marten. This is a cat-like animal with short legs, a tail almost as long as the body, and with a pointed snout, rather like a mongoose's. It is a variegated brown, black and yellow above, paler below, and with a prominent yellow throat. The northern representative of this marten is found throughout the Himalayan range from the tropical foothills right up to 9000 ft or so, in the temperate zone, being particularly at home in the humid eastern Himalayas. South of the Himalayas, this animal is not found at all until we reach the Nilgiris, over 1000 miles away, where again appears the very closely related Nilgiri Marten (*Charronia gwatkinsii*). So closely related is it, in fact, that until fairly recently the two were considered identical. It is deep brown from head to rump, the forequarters being almost reddish, and also has the characteristic yellow throat. This species keeps to the higher, more temperate portions of the Nilgiris above about 3000 ft elevation, and is also found in the Coorg and Travancore hills. Yellowthroated Martens are largely carnivorous, but will also eat fruits and berries. They are bold and active and hunt at night as well as by day, on the ground as well as in trees. In spite of their small size, they sometimes kill young barking deer. They are adept at climbing trees and hunt squirrels and birds in the treetops, also rob birds' nests of their eggs and young. On one occasion in Sikkim I heard a terrific commotion among birds and could see on the next hill in the distance a swarm of largish black birds flying agitatedly about a lofty treetop. On investigation the cause was revealed to be a marten running along the topmost boughs in search of prey, being angrily and noisily chivvied by the largest gathering of Haircrested Drongos I have ever come across. This bird is not usually gregarious to such an extent. In this clamorous rabble there were well over fifty individuals, assisted vigorously by several other bird species of the neighbourhood, all intent on swearing and hurling execrations on the marauder who seemed to be quite unperturbed by the demonstrations.

Another obvious relict of the Himalayan fauna found in the Nilgiris and the southernmost section of the Western Ghats is the Nilgiri Tahr, popularly known as "ibex" among European sportsmen. This wild goat, which lives on the precipitous slopes of the Nilgiris and adjoining southern hills at heights of between 4000 and 6000 ft, has a similarly broken or discontinuous distribution to the Yellowthroated Marten. Its nearest northern cousin is the Himalayan Tahr found throughout the Himalayas from the Pir Panjal to Sikkim, also living in similarly precipitous terrain of towering cliffs, dense scrub, and forest.

The Nilgiri Tahr is separate from its northern congener by at least a thousand miles of country which at the present day is totally unsuited to its existence. The only explanation for these far-flung colonies is that at some remote period in the geological history of India, conditions from the Himalayas to the Nilgiris were uniform enough for the Tahr to have had a continuous distribution. Natural causes produced a change in the intervening country; with them the Tahr either retreated towards the ends of the chain or died out. Therefore, what we now see in south India are virtually marooned populations of Himalayan origin. An analysis of pertinent factors suggests that the connection between the Himalayas and the south Indian hills in former times existed from somewhere in the region of Sikkim over the Satpura trend of mountains across continental India to the northern tip of the Western Ghats in the region of Khandesh, and thence down the western side of the peninsula. Erosion has worn down the connecting chain of mountainous country until it no longer retained its significance as a rain-catching factor in relation to the South West monsoon. The decreased rainfall and humidity brought about changes in the vegetation and climate which were no longer suitable to the specialised humid forest living forms and that these either retreated to more suitable areas or perished, leaving the isolated population at either end. A comparative study of the fauna and flora of Sikkim and those of the humid Malabar zone is one of the most interesting and fruitful subjects for an investigator of the geography of Indian animals and plants.

On the whole, Sikkim is rather poor in the larger mammals. It is believed that the immense trade in furs in the comparatively recent past may be partly responsible for this state of affairs. Most of the furs that now come from Sikkim, actually originate from beyond its borders in Tibet. Tiger, panther, snow leopard, golden cat, and some of the other unusual species of wild cats are still to be found, but they are very rare.

The Himalayan Black Bear occurs in small numbers at fairly high elevations and up to the level of tree growth, living chiefly on wild fruits, roots, and tubers. It descends to the lower valleys in winter and causes occasional depredations among livestock. The majority of the animals, however, go into the winter sleep or hibernation in some secluded cave, and emerge only with the first signs of returning spring. Wolves are found in the northern parts, beyond Lachung and Thangu, and do a certain amount of damage among the sheep that are taken up to the Alpine pastures for grazing in summer.

Mammals in the wild state are far more difficult to study in the field than are birds, for example, or many of the other groups of animals. For one thing they are largely nocturnal in their habits, and spend the daytime in the seclusion of their lairs and in thickets. Most of the larger animals like deer are subject to constant harassment and persecution by human beings for meat and other marketable products, and can seldom be watched and studied in their natural undisturbed state. All the information we have concerning their life histories is largely the result of pieced together scraps of information supplied by sportsmen and trappers, chiefly of a circumstantial nature, and it must be admitted that on the whole our knowledge of the habits of mammals is woefully meagre and deficient. We know little concerning even those species which live in more or less close contact with human beings and are often locally destructive to crops and in other ways. So little, indeed, do we know about the interdependence of animals upon one another, or upon their physical environment and the true place they occupy in the balance of nature, that man has repeatedly found cause to repent his folly in either trying to exterminate certain species believed to be harmful to his interests, or by the introduction of outwardly beneficial ones to control the numbers of seemingly harmful ones. The killing off of deer and pig in certain parts of Madhya Pradesh some years ago, either for commercial gain or as a measure of crop protection, had the disastrous effect of turning the tigers of those areas into man-eaters owing to the deprivation of their natural prey. Mongoose, introduced from India into Mauritius for keeping the rat population down in the sugar plantation areas, did their work most efficiently; but having done so, they turned their attentions to the poultry of the farmers and on the native wild birds. The ravages the mongoose ultimately caused were far more disastrous than those of the rats for whose control it was introduced. When our politicians hold forth so glibly on the folly of preserving wild animals which palpably do some damage to crops, and loudly advocate their total extermination, they unfortunately only display their ignorance of the finely balanced interplay that exists among God's creatures, any radical disturbance of which may bring perhaps unsuspected disaster.

One of the most characteristic and interesting animals of Sikkim and the eastern Himalayas, extending into Upper Burma and South China, is the Cat-Bear or Little Panda (*Ailurus fulgens*). It is seldom seen during daytime, but judging from the numbers that are always on sale in the Calcutta animal market it would appear to be not a particularly rare species. This animal has lately come in for a great deal of publicity through the example kept as a pet by our prime minister. The Little Panda is a thick-furred animal, well named "cat-bear" since it resembles both these. It is an attractive creature, bright chestnut in overall colouration with white markings on the face, a stumpy muzzle, and a long bushy tail with dark rings round it. Animals that live solitary lives and are not social usually possess some means by which they can discover the whereabouts of others of their kind, particularly of the opposite sex, for mating, and so on. This panda has a gland under the tail which produces a strong odour when the animal is excited. In captivity it has been observed to rub this glandular area against the surface over which it moved, leaving a "scent trail" which may well serve as the means by which two solitary individuals are brought together.

Perhaps the commonest species amongst the carnivore of Sikkim is the Large Indian Civet, *Viverra zibetha*, a sturdily built mongoose-like animal with short stumpy legs and a long bushy tail, banded black and white. It is dark hoary grey in colour with irregular dark bands and faint rosettes. It is a nocturnal animal and therefore seldom seen, but its presence is usually felt by its depredations on poultry, which are often quite considerable. It hunts birds and small animals, including snakes and frogs, and supplements its diet with berries, fruits, and vegetable matter.

The Civets derive their English name from the Arabic "zabat" a term applied to the scent derived from a gland situated under the tail. It is a strong and evil-smelling discharge whose function seems to be to repel enemies when the animal is cornered, and doubtless also serves to advertise the presence of individuals to their own kind. Strangely enough the malodorous secretion from this gland, highly diluted, is used in the manufacture of perfumery and for medicinal purposes, and fetches high prices.

A spate of mountaineering expeditions from foreign lands has recently deluged India in attempts to conquer Everest and some of his intractable Himalayan brethren. One of the stock items in newspapermen's interviews with the returned mountaineers inevitably concerns the Abominable Snowman. In view of this, and the widespread interest this mysterious being holds for the public, mention of the Himalayan Langur (*Presbytis schistaceus* Hodge.) must on no account be omitted from a list of the animals of Sikkim. The Himalayan Langur is a much larger and more heavily built animal than its familiar cousin, the Hanuman monkey of the plains. It is fairly plentiful in the Lachen Valley between 5000 and 10,000 ft and confined to heavy forest.

It will be remembered that not so long ago someone at the British Museum in London expressed the opinion that the photograph of enormous human-like footprints seen in the snow at high altitudes, recently brought back by one of these expeditions – attributed by the more imaginative to the Abominable Snowman – were in fact these of a Himalayan Langur. Others have, perhaps with greater reasonableness, considered such footprints to be left by the Himalayan Brown Bear. To everybody acquainted with the Himalayan Langur in its wild state, the latest theory seems as fantastic as it is improbable. Although it emanates from an august scientific institution like the British Museum, one can only hope that it was not intended to be taken too seriously. Besides the fact that a Langur's footprints cannot be conceived to equal those of an oversized human, there seems no earthly reason whatever why a langur – a forest-haunting, tree-climbing, four-footed creature, whose food consists mainly of fruits and leaves gathered in the treetops – should forsake its accustomed habitat to undertake an excursion so far above the limit of tree growth, walking over snow-covered ground and presumably in the thoroughly unlangur-like upright position of a biped. It is also difficult to understand why the langur, which normally lives in troops and family parties, should isolate himself so completely when venturing forth on his mountaineering jaunts – for solitary is how the Snowman evidently travels.

No. We must try again for a more convincing answer.

4

Man and Nature in India: The Ecological Balance*

IT IS A MATTER OF some satisfaction to all of us interested in the conservation of Nature that there is now, at last, a growing awareness and interest in India in the preservation of wildlife and wild places. What is now required is the understanding of the fact that human ecology is an integral part of Nature conservation, and all who take a total view of life on earth must realise that man's future cannot be considered separately from that of other life. From the time that man became an agriculturist and husbandman, thereby enabling himself to overcome the natural constraints that had kept the numbers of his predecessor – the hunter and forager – within the environmental capacity, man's impact on his environment has been largely disastrous. As examples one could consider that Cradle of Civilisation, the Middle East, now largely, arid, as a monument to man's misuse of the land. A number of ancient civilisations seem to have culminated in deserts in the same way – Egypt, the kingdoms of the Middle East, Carthage, and the Indus Valley civilisation. All seem to have gone to ruin down the same drain. None had profited from the knowledge of earlier disasters. Unhappily, the same sorry process continues today, only that improvements in communications and technology now permit man to exercise his expertise as a creator of deserts on a global scale and at a more accelerated tempo.

As far as forests and wildlife are concerned there can be hardly any doubt that we in India have been living prodigally off an abundant capital. A study on any endangered natural resource shows that the basic problem in every case, and invariably, is the ever-increasing – "exploding" is the right word – human population, leading to a constant erosion of that resource. In an article in the *Journal of the Bombay Natural History Society* M.S. Randhawa provides historical evidence to prove that in the last two thousand years there has been a progressive desiccation of northern India. As an example he cites the changes that have occurred in the Mathura region of Uttar Pradesh. That area apparently once received over 2000 mm of rainfall as against the present 600 mm. The evidence on which Randhawa bases his thesis is mainly the sculptures of the period, and specific references in the Puranas to the Asoka tree (*Saraca asoca*), and other moisture-loving plant species whose present-day distribution is restricted to areas with over 2000 mm rainfall. Thus the Mathura region appears to have degraded within historical times from an area capable of supporting luxuriant forests to one with a semi-desert type of vegetation, rather similar to that of the Rajasthan desert.

The loss in the productivity of the land and the consequent degradation of the environment is nowhere more clearly shown than in the history of some of our endangered species of wildlife. The distribution of the Great Indian Rhinoceros sufficiently illustrates this point. This ponderous animal, now restricted to the swampy riverain forests of a few sanctuaries in Assam, W. Bengal, and Nepal, was found in historic times from Peshawar – where the Mughal Emperor Humayun hunted it – eastward across the Gangetic Plain to Assam. The fact that the rhinoceros requires a swampy grass jungle to exist is a pointer to the conditions then obtaining in areas which are now practically desert. The Pink-headed Duck, another resident of the same swampy forest habitat, became extinct in the '30s of the present century. Loss of its habitat, combined with the fact that it nested on the ground among reeds and not up in tree holes like our other resident ducks, is possibly one of the main reasons for the disappearance of the species. The distribution of the lion in this country is perhaps further evidence of the result of man-made environmental changes. The widespread extension in the range of the lion – an inhabitant of dry habitats – in N. India was possibly correlated with the withdrawal of moist conditions in the Indo-Gangetic Plain. This was the result of large-scale clearing of the forests as more and more land was brought under cultivation for an ever-increasing human population. The lion itself eventually fell a victim to the rising population pressure, losing its habitat to cultivation.

Habitat destruction is the primary reason for the disappearance or rarity of most of our wildlife, and under present conditions there seems every likelihood that the process of destruction will continue. It is, indeed, a tragic situation. There is not enough land for all the land-hungry, and much of the land that is now being cleared under population pressure – some of it magnificent primeval evergreen forest – will surely be abandoned in a permanently ruined state – another martyr to human irresponsibility! It would appear that what is really needed is not more land for cultivation but better utilisation of the land that is already under cultivation.

The disappearance of the rhinoceros, the lion, or the tiger are examples striking enough to attract wide attention even of the layman, but there is a considerable invisible loss which by nature of its obscureness seldom comes to notice. One example of such is the loss suffered by the agricultural economy of the country due to the thoughtless destruction of the predators of agricultural pests. And hardly any voice is raised in protest. The reptile skin trade, running into hundreds of tons annually – happily banned at last – effectively removed snakes and lizards which are amongst the most stringent natural checks on rats and other rodent crop-pests. Similarly the trade in frogs' legs removes one of the important regulators of the population of harmful insects and other small animals. One observable effect of this commercial exploitation of frogs is the marked increase in land crab (*Paratelphusa* sp.) which destroys paddy seedlings, and whose numbers were kept in check by frogs. Due to superstitious prejudice and ill-founded allegations against owls and the diurnal birds of prey, man axes his own legs, as it were. Their senseless destruction deprives agriculture and forestry of the services of some of man's staunchest allies in the ceaseless battle against the fecund tribe of rats, and other scourges like the locust.

In recent years advanced technology has, paradoxically enough, added dangerously to the hazards to wildlife and environments by the introduction of chemical pesticides and herbicides in the campaign to grow more food for the burgeoning human population. By the poisonous pollution these have brought about of water, earth, and air, they are boomeranging on Man himself. Whatever conservation measures are now undertaken, or may be undertaken in the future, can be expected to function as no more than stop-gaps, and no permanent remedy for the ecological imbalance can be devised unless and until the human population is effectively contained.

This then is the problem. Unless man is able to discipline himself there is no hope of avoiding the ecological disaster towards which he is rapidly heading. In order to restore and regulate the ecological balance conservation now demands that the human population be drastically controlled, not only for the wise use of the available natural resources but for the very existence of man himself. To find the remedies one must examine the causes. The evolution of man, unlike that of other animals has, above all, been the evolution of his brain. This is what has enabled him to overcome the limitations natural to other animals. He meets and deals with his environment at two levels: firstly, the intellectual, aided by the vast area of knowledge available to him because of his intellect, and secondly the physical level in which he is in no way different from other animals. His reproductive capacity lies in the second plane, and to control it the approach should be through knowledge of the reproductive function of other animals. To this end fruitful research could be undertaken on the factors that cause seasonal reproductive behaviour in other animals, and whether it would be possible to permanently extend the inhibitory forces. On the face of it this does not seem an impossible task since, in reverse, we have succeeded in breaking down the seasonal inhibitory force in domestic animals. For instance the Red Junglefowl – the ancestor of our domestic poultry – has, unlike the latter, a fixed and limited breeding season in nature. It is a curious fact, but true, that in truly social insects such as ants and bees the majority of individuals are sterile; thus there is a built-in population control mechanism in the community. Can this model not be emulated by humans?

Whatever method we employ, the intellectual or the physical or a combination of both, time is running out for man. He must realise that his body, like that of other animals, is subject to narrow physical and chemical constraints and that, however intellectually versatile he may be, he could become a victim of ecological disaster just as any other animal if he refuses to pay heed to the warnings of a misused natural system working under fixed natural laws. To us in India especially, this is the Writing on the Wall.

Index

(Page numbers of the Hindustani radio talk numbered 3a in the Contents have not been included)